THE AUTOBIOGRAPHY OF AN APARTMENT HOUSE

Larsen, Flynn, 1971-
The Autobiography of an Apartment House
ISBN: 978-0-6159823-9-7
Library of Congress Control Number: 2014906133

The Apartment House Press
74 Rombout Avenue
Beacon, New York, NY 12508
www.oliveropenpress.com

Design: William van Roden
williamvanroden.com

THE AUTOBIOGRAPHY OF AN APARTMENT HOUSE

PHOTOGRAPHY BY FLYNN LARSEN

TEXT BY ERIC LARSEN

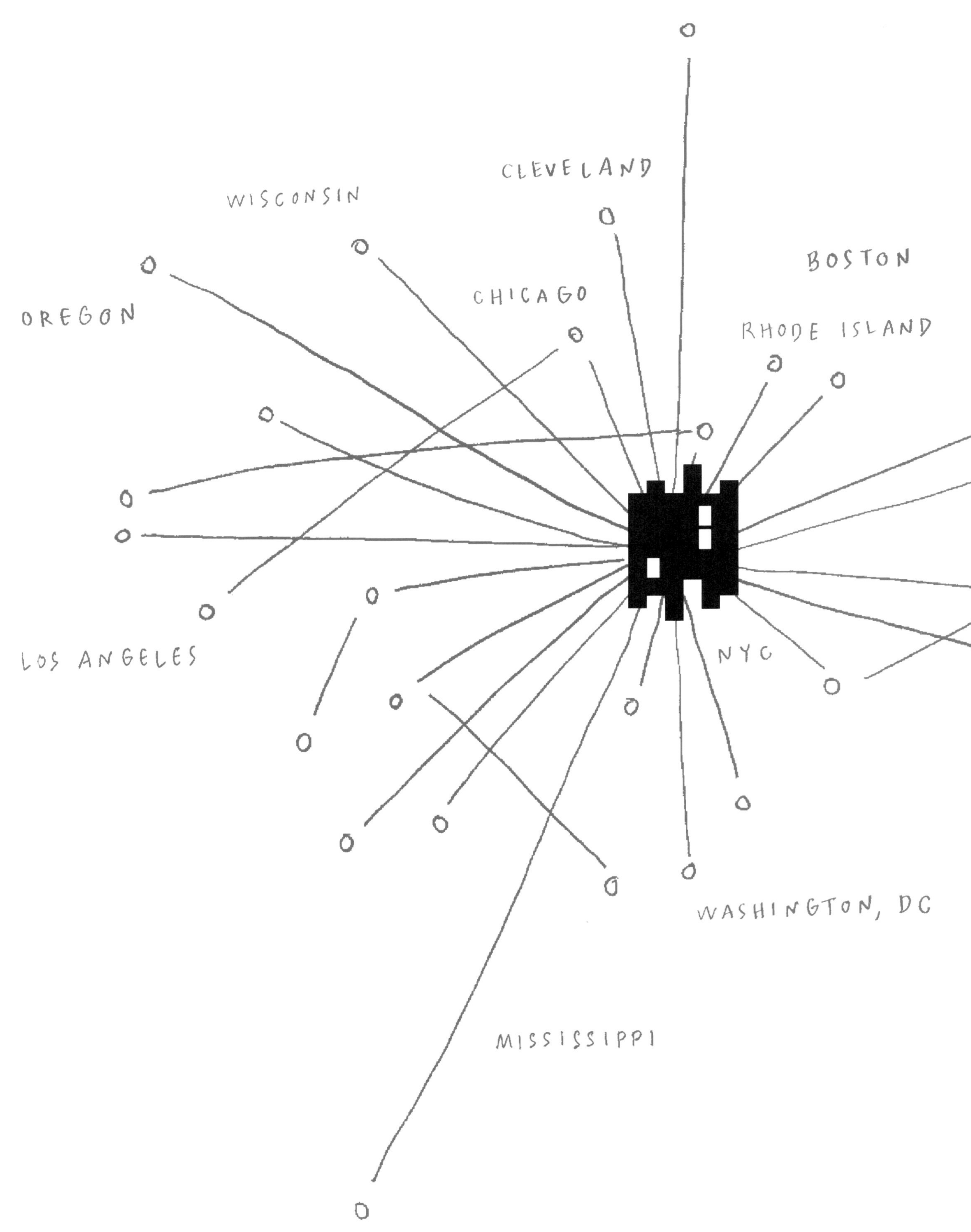

CLEVELAND
WISCONSIN
BOSTON
OREGON
CHICAGO
RHODE ISLAND
LOS ANGELES
NYC
WASHINGTON, DC
MISSISSIPPI

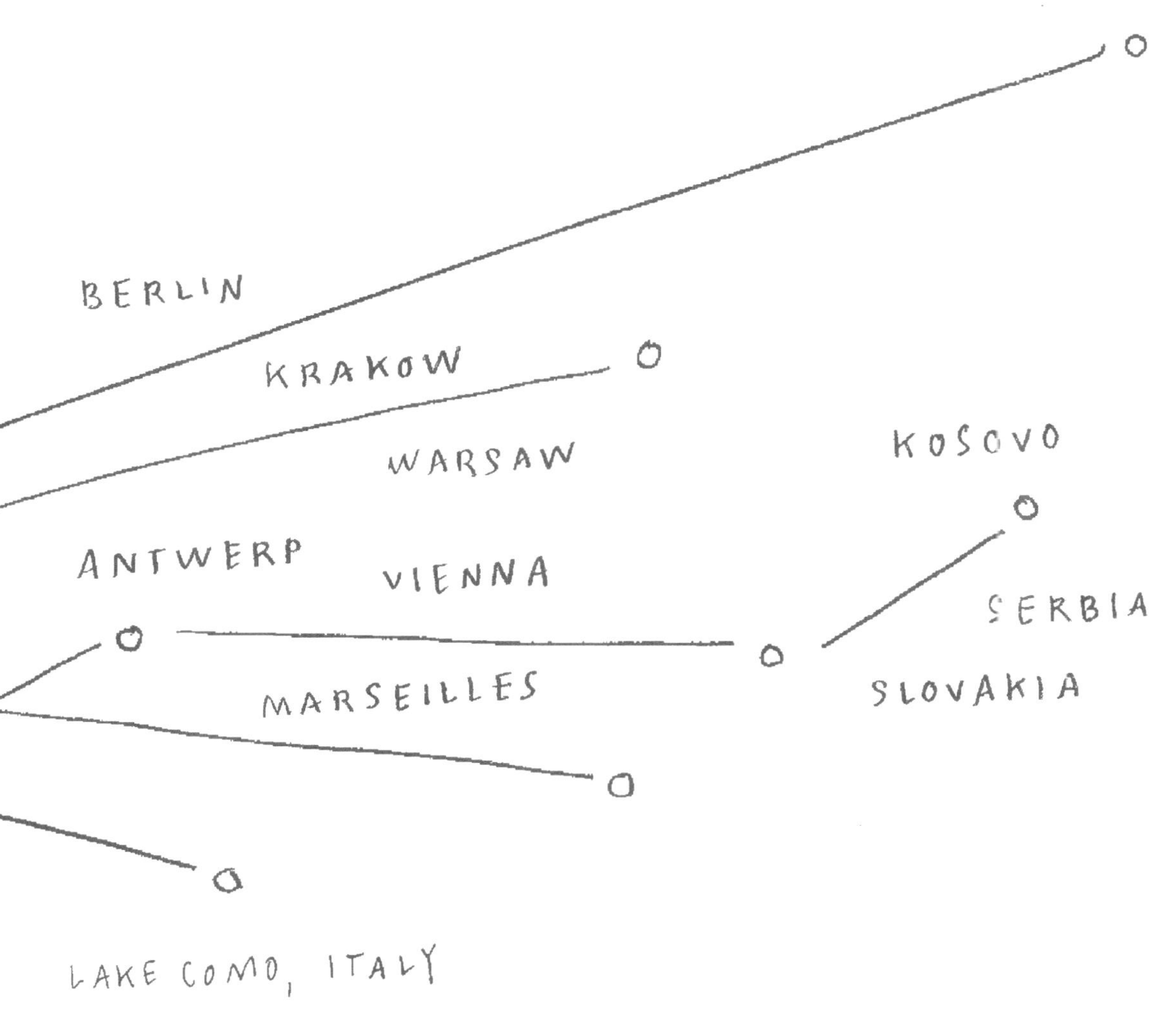

Tess crossed the continent to reach apartment 6D...

TABLE OF CONTENTS

They left like swallows,
quietly and quickly,
and they left a very deep
emptiness behind them.

THE AUTOBIOGRAPHY OF AN APARTMENT HOUSE

AN INTRODUTION

The dead man himself
appeared one night —
and then left,
taking with him beds,
tables, lamps, every last
stick of furniture.

1

If buildings could talk, what would they say? If they could listen, see, remember—what would we hear from them?

THIS IS A QUESTION common to anyone who's ever gone in search of "history." Anyone who has visited Gettysburg knows the frustrating and spell-binding experience of wondering, if that ancient field of woe could talk, what it would possibly say.

"Ancient." The very word, along with its non-adjective fellow, "antiquity," brings a sense of mysterious and tantalizing silence—the same thing Keats must have been feeling in "Ode on a Grecian Urn" when he wrote the lines about "silence and slow time." Anyone who has strolled around the Acropolis, or has gazed up into Brunelleschi's dome, or stared dumbfounded at the Traitor's Gate in the Tower of London, or stood in the warmth of an autumn breeze at Little Big Horn—every one of those people has wondered what it would be like if the places, things, objects, and structures left from the past could talk.

It doesn't have to be so very "ancient," either, for the magic question to be awakened—you can be seized by it in the sea-side quietness of Skara Brae, the Neolithic village in Orkney, Scotland, that's five thousand years old. Or you can be seized by it on a stage-door tour of Radio City Music Hall, the great New York City shrine that dates all the way back to a distant 1932.

Or the magic question can grab you from, well, let's say 1925. That was the year when the apartment house I live in—the one that inspired this book—was built. Three-quarters of a century ago plus thirteen years—as of this writing—for a grand total of eighty-eight. That's how far back we'll be going in this, our own, study of silence and slow time.

The house we live in isn't yet a century old, but it still holds somewhere within it the old days of coal chutes in the sidewalks, striped awnings over the apartment windows, and big square black Packards rolling up to the front door. Its beginning in 1925 wasn't too late for it to have seen the itinerant knife-grinder, fruit seller, rag man. Every story, sound, object, event, and change in mood is still harbored somewhere within the spirit of the house. The Depression years, the pre-war years, the war years of few cars in the streets, of U-boat scares, dim-outs, and shades drawn over evening windows. Through the close of the 1940s and into the early years of the new decade, the building was still spared the omnipresence of air conditioning, and on warm evenings, through open windows, tenants could hear musicians practicing all around the neighborhood. In the apartments themselves, reading lamps were still the center of focus during the evening hours, and the building's occupants still sat beside them, still sat in comfortable chairs and couch-corners under their light, still spent time in the quaint reading of newspapers, magazines, books, catalogues, pamphlets, letters—until, all of a sudden, the building's roof sprouted a Ben Shahn thicket of television aerials, and the whole nation underwent a change outwardly and began dying inwardly.

In 1971, when I (me, the person writing these words) and my wife moved in, the building was still four years short of being half a century old. We had been married for six years, and shortly after we became tenants, our first child joined us. That baby grew up in the building and is now the adult who has taken the photographs in this book. Compiling the book was her idea in the first place, as a way of chronicling at least some part of the building's life by assembling a portrait portfolio of its tenants. The story of a building, after all, is the story of the lives inside it, those present, those past, and even, or so we trust, those yet to come.

No photographer, however, can take pictures of those who aren't there. As a result, Flynn and I agreed that I would write an "introduction" trying to convey some sense of the building and its past, based on my—our—four decades as tenants. The portraits, in turn, would "speak" about those who are living here in the present, or who were living here at the time the photographs were taken. As for the future, we can only pray that it remain well enough valued so that at least some of us will still be here when it comes around, in its own good time, to check and see.

Flynn's sister was born three years after we moved in. For the next fifteen years we remained a family of four, until Flynn graduated from high school and left for college. Gavin finished high school in 1992 and left home to take up a career in dance. Both, of course, came back from time to time; the building was still "home," as it remained for another decade or so—and in certain ways still does. Before we moved to New York, neither my wife nor I had ever lived in one place for as long as the eighteen years that Flynn and Gavin each lived in this one. Now, of course, for Anne and me, the stretch extends past forty years.

Flynn moved back into her old room for a year or so beginning in 2000, and Gavin did the same—and into the same room—two or three years later, when she was between companies. These extended returns home sometimes coincided with other important markers. Flynn's year, for example, coincided with what everyone now calls, simply, "9/11." And Gavin's coincided with the death of one of the building's longest-term tenants.

In 2001 or 2002, the tenant whom we all spoke of—quite incorrectly—as "Mrs. Engel" passed away. I'm certain that Mrs. Engel's tenancy covered a longer span than anyone else's in the building's history. She moved in thirty years earlier than we did, arriving at the building in 1941, with her father the rabbi. I don't know if there was still a mother at that time, but I lean toward believing that there was. The family managed to leave Europe before the Nazis closed off escape. Where they came from, exactly, I don't know. I wish I did.

When I met her, I would guess Mrs. Engel to have been in her middle forties, or possibly older. I was born in 1941, the year Mrs. Engel moved into the apartment house, and certainly she was twenty years older than me. At the very least, when I was thirty, in 1971, she was fifty or perhaps fifty-five. Thirty years later, in 2001, she would have been eighty or eighty-five. By this reckoning, either way, she died in her eighties.

For slightly more than three decades we lived two floors directly up and down from one another, we on the higher and she on the lower floor, and yet we became familiar enough with one another only to exchange amenities or make small talk in the elevator. Still, Mrs. Engel must have felt at least some degree of trust beyond what simple good manners can generate (admittedly, I did make a point always of being polite with her), or she wouldn't have chosen me as someone—or as the one—to trust with her mail. I imagine that she thought of me as a "nice young man," one she could trust because he was polite, had two young daughters, and taught something-or-other in college.

In any case—and of course I was happy to do it—the favor consisted of taking in Mrs. Engel's mail while she was away on her annual two-week summer vacation. This vacation of Mrs. Engel's seemed to me exotic by merit of its being so old-fashioned. She would go to a resort hotel on the Atlantic shore, where she would socialize with friends, stroll around the hotel environs, take in the sea air from any of the rocking chairs that lined the veranda, and, of course, gather in the common dining room for meals three times each day. The place that offered this old-world, European-style, genteel, easeful getaway was no farther afield than—Brooklyn.

In other words, Mrs. Engel took her vacation at a place she could have reached by subway if she had chosen. The fact is, though, that a car came by the building to pick her up.

I wonder if this sojourn may have been a family tradition, a genteel retreat to an old and European-style hotel, something that Mrs. Engel had done long ago, with her own parents. I don't know. Some things, though, I do know. At some point before we moved into the building, Mrs. Engel's parents had both disappeared. I know—from my years of small talk with Mrs. Engel—that in 1941 the building had been attended not only by a super and a porter, but also by a doorman and an elevator man. Both of the latter, Mrs. Engel insisted many, many times, wore white gloves.

Could it be that our unglamorous, homely, and often unkempt building had once been that well-attended and gracious? I don't know. I know that Mrs. Engel told me, many times, that the doorman and the elevator man had worn white gloves.

When she left her apartment, even just to go to the Broadway shops, Mrs. Engel would put on lipstick, rouge her cheeks, and get into her usual black coat, which came a hands' breadth below the knees and which she wore with its buttons done up even in the hottest weather. I can't help but think that Mrs. Engel lived in a pocket of time. Her habits, at least the outside ones, were those appropriate to a young girl of respectable family going out in public on the streets of Warsaw or Vienna in, say, 1910 or 1915.

She was old-fashioned, not fancy. On the Upper West Side of the early 1970s, she was still one of many—just another aging European woman, most likely living alone, probably a widow, on the timid side in manner but not—yet—frumpy, helpless, or shabby. I doubt that she was at all well off, though I also suspect she very likely did have enough money to see her through to the end. Of the mail I collected for her, a considerable amount came from large corporations. Mrs. Engel, shareholder? It seemed so. Equally intriguing, however, was the way her non-financial mail was addressed. A good part of it came directly to her, but a generous share, easily half of it, came not to Mrs. Engel at all, but, instead, to her father.

Fliers, announcements, brochures, and varieties of business letters were addressed to Dr. David Engel, or to Rabbi David Engel, or to Dr. D. Engel, or Rabbi D. Engel. They were never addressed simply to David Engel or to Mr. David Engel.

That is all I know of Mrs. Engel's father. But I also know that his daughter, from at least 1971, and likely much earlier, on into the beginning of the new century, allowed—or caused—it to be thought in many quarters that he was still alive.

I didn't begin taking in Mrs. Engel's mail until sometime in the mid or even late 1980s. Until then, there were a good number of other people in the building whom Mrs. Engel would have relied on before turning to me.

One by one, however, these others left the building. Mr. and Mrs. Weilberg, for example, directly below Mrs. Engel, moved to another part of town—on the east side—as soon as their youngest son (of three) started college. Jacob Ernst died and, in that way, departed from the building also. Long before Jacob Ernst's death, over a decade earlier, Mrs. Keflick, the dour woman on Mrs. Engel's own floor, had moved away after her own husband, the Australian, died. Of Mrs. Engel's several old familiars, only Mrs. Temkin lingered on, all the way—though shrinking all the while—until 2009.

I don't know Mrs. Keflick's story, where in Europe she came from or when she moved into the building. She was there when we came, I know, with her Australian husband whom, to Flynn and Gavin's amusement, I privately referred to as Mr. Big Nose. I liked him well enough, although a rumor persisted that he was in the habit of exposing himself in the elevator, something never corroborated with any authority sufficient to make me believe it. Whether he drank, I don't know for a fact, but his immense nose, and a good area of the face adjacent to it, was positively alive with a vividly red pattern made of tiny veins and broken capillaries. His Chaucerian appearance aside, I enjoyed meeting him in the elevator, partly because small talk gave me the pleasure of hearing his Australian accent. He wasn't what anyone would call a cheerful man, exactly, although in my own knowledge of him he was well-met and certainly affable enough. In these traits, he could hardly have been more unlike his poor wife, whose sour face wore a permanent mask of the most woeful glumness, depression, and joylessness imaginable. Her face seemed to hang down almost as if it were slipping off of itself, while her mouth also was perpetually downturned. Her drooping eyes looked as expressionless, sad, and woebegone as a bloodhound's. I never saw her smile. I never heard her laugh. I never saw her look the least bit happy. It may well be, thinking back, that I never saw a sign of responsiveness in her of any kind at all.

A person wonders what horrors she may have seen to leave her in such a state. On the other hand, though, such morbid dourness could simply have been her natural character from the start. But then that thought, in its own turn, makes a person wonder how Mrs. Keflick ever managed to snag Mr. Keflick, or how he, for that matter, had ever been drawn enough to her in the first place so as to get even within wooing distance.

We'll never know.

One day I left the apartment on an errand of one kind or another. The elevator stopped on six, the door opened, and in came Mr. Keflick. I could see that he was in discomfort, and he told me so as well. "Pains," he said. "Bad." He kept one hand pressed against his stomach, hard enough so as to indent it, his fingers spread out. In his other hand he held a folded handkerchief. Every few seconds, he drew it across his brow. He looked awful.

The super was outside the front door—by arrangement, as it turned out. Mr. Keflick switched his handkerchief from right hand to left and from his right pocket drew out two keys on a ring and gave them to the super. This super was "Mr. Hernandez," the first super we'd had during our time in the building and the last super to be called "Mr." The Age of First Names was beginning. My guess is that the year was 1975 or 1976.

The keys were Mr. Keflick's car keys. What he seemed concerned about more than anything was that Mr. Hernandez would take care of parking the car on alternate sides of the street in accordance with the street-cleaning rules. Yes, Mr. Hernandez said. Don't forget, Mr. Keflick said. I'll do it, Mr. Hernandez said. I've got to go to the doctor, Mr. Keflick said. He directed this last remark to me rather than to Mr. Hernandez, who apparently knew it already. Too preoccupied to give any more attention to his manners, Mr. Keflick simply turned toward Broadway without another word. He walked bent forward very slightly, not his customary posture.

I don't remember watching him hail a cab, if he did. I only remember watching him walk toward Broadway. There was a sort of shuffle in his gait, as though it hurt to move his feet up and down, so that he was trying to slide them along on the sidewalk.

Whatever poor Mr. Keflick had must have been very, very bad. That morning was the last time I ever saw him in my life. Or in his, for that matter.

His wife moved out almost immediately after he died. She must have found a place farther downtown, since from time to time afterward I would see her in the Argo diner at 90th and Broadway. In those days, the Argo was a major gathering place for European widows. Around three o'clock on weekdays you would find them there in groups of three or four, sometimes five or six, sipping coffee and talking among themselves over mountainous wedges of the Argo's cream-filled layer cakes. Some years earlier, they would have patronized the delicatessens instead of the Greek diners. But by this time, the sit-down delis in the neighborhood, with their waiters dressed in black, had already disappeared, and so for these aging women the Argo had to stand in for the familiar old cafés and Delikatessens and Konditoreis they had known in Berlin, or Krakow, or Warsaw, or Vienna, or any of the other hundreds of places they'd been driven from.

Among these women, as I said, I would sometimes see Mrs. Keflick, sitting in a staring silence, as if catatonic with gloom and loss and despair amid the low-pitched but animated conversation of those all around her.

This population of women also changed, as, along with it, the entire Upper West Side changed. In the early seventies there were still rows of park-benches on the islands in the middle of Broadway. At 86th Street, for example, there were four or five rows on the south tip of the northern island and four or five on the north tip of the southern, these two, almost like theater sections, facing one another across the width of 86th Street. On warm days in good weather, the benches would be filled up with elderly people, European émigrés almost to a one. Then, year by year, you could see the change in this population almost literally as it was taking place. First went the husbands and old men, one by one, with nobody coming to replace them. Then the numbers of the widows began to dwindle, then to decline rapidly, until it was almost as if none of them had ever existed. In later years, the theater-tiers of benches were torn out and replaced by a single park bench on each spot.

In the fall of 1971, during Sukkot, tenants in our building put up a house of branches, twigs, and bits of shrubbery in what we called then and still call "the east courtyard," though a more accurate term would be the "east air shaft." Nevertheless, late one afternoon as I came home from class, I heard singing and looked down from inside one of the lobby windows. There it was, the Sukkot hut, built by my own neighbors, who were gathered there now, praying and singing.

When I spent the academic year 1964–65 in Madison, Wisconsin, I lived, with four other graduate students, in rooms on the top two floors of an old frame house in a semi-derelict part of town. The owner lived on the ground floor and shared a name with one of the people in this book—Mrs. Temkin. On Friday mornings during that fall, the first Mrs. Temkin would bake something for Shabbat—what it was, I don't know, but the scent of it would come up the interior staircase and into our rooms. There was onion in it, I'm sure, along with other smells I couldn't identify. My roommates gagged, made bad jokes, held their noses on their way downstairs. But I liked the smell. It seemed to me like a doorway into a far-distant past that was beyond retrieving other than through this scent.

In New York, I smelled the same thing only a handful of times, in the autumns of our earliest few years. As for the Sukkot hut, that first example was also the last I saw. Changes came fast. We had arrived at one of the last moments that was still overlapping with the Jewish history that had touched the building, or that had all but filled it. There may have been other Sukkot huts, but I never saw one again.

We started our own life in the building just as the lives of many others there were drawing toward their ends. Things are much different now, but in the autumn of 1971 not a single pet dog lived in any apartment, and, as for children, there were only three, all boys. One of these was the youngest of the three sons of the Weilbergs, the son whose entry into college six or seven years later was the trigger for his parents to move out of the building.

The other two were brothers, one six years old and the other seven, handsome, good-featured kids with wavy hair. Their mother was a tall, slim, and beautiful woman with a long neck and Giacometti-like head who, perhaps not surprisingly, operated a ballet school. Both of her sons took class with her, and both appeared professionally in performances of *The Nutcracker* and *A Midsummer Night's Dream*. The question-mark in the family was the father, Charlie Vogel. A failed actor, then a stage hand, and finally a member of the stage hands' union, he was a short, solid, handsome man with an attractively rugged face who, when he put on pressed pants and a tweed jacket, looked ready for anything from *On the Waterfront* to The Metropolitan Opera. But something awful was knotted up inside him, a ganglion of darkness.

Whether the origins of his anger lay in frustration and disappointment, I don't know, but everyone in the building knew that any single moment could throw him off the rails and into the likeness of a raging bull. With lots to drink or without a drop, he could fly into great outbursts of rage. His voice was a powerful baritone, and his curses and threats would rise up through the west courtyard into all the apartment windows when he was venting his rage at Damara, or, willy-nilly, at Topher or Nate, or even at the three of them together. There were periods of calm between outrages but never an end to them, and in good time Damara gave up and left Charlie, taking the boys with her—although by then they were getting nearly old enough to begin their own wanderings.

For a lengthy period of time after Damara left, there was quiet. But then Charlie remarried—or at least a very pretty, very slight, very frail Spanish-speaking young woman named Teresa moved in, and Charlie introduced her to people as his wife. And then the dreadful spiral began all over again. The guttural, inchoate roars would leap from Charlie's throat and fly up the airshaft, seeming louder even than before and certainly more frequent. In a new development, the bellow-ing was often accompanied by the noise of breaking dishware. These were horrendous sounds. Tenants called 911, police cars pulled up in front, officers went to Charlie's door. Like Damara, Maria left him, although whether she had any place to go for shelter, no one knew In the years after Teresa's departure, Charlie, left alone, trudged gradually to an end. His health went bad. He walked bent forward, then with a cane, finally scarcely able to shuffle his way to the grocery store and back. His rough good looks drooped into the haggard face of an old man. He disappeared for varying lengths of time—only the super seemed to know where went—and returned. He couldn't have been much older than I was, but there came a time, on those occasions when I would stop to talk with him on the street, that he had to stare at me blankly for a minute or two before he could remember who I was.

After he died, his apartment remained empty and locked up for a considerable time—nothing inside except furniture, clothing, possessions, and silence. Then one day two young men appeared at our apartment door. It took more than just a second or two for me to realize that these tall, handsome, strapping men were Topher and Nate. Not all of their luck had been good, by any means, after they'd left home with their mother, abandoning Charlie's wretched life to go however it could. They had, nevertheless, kept an eye on him in a variety of ways, and they also knew that I had made some few efforts to help their father in small ways from time to time. Now that they were here to empty out his apartment, they'd stopped by to extend me their thanks.

They were, as I said, tall, strapping, handsome young men. Polite, self-assured, well-spoken, poised—they were like trees, strong, upright, and confident. Even I was proud of them. They were no relatives to me, and I hadn't known them at all well when, as early-teenagers, they left the building. But I knew, now, that they had managed to grow strong and straight, even out of the bad soil of their poor father's wretched life.

Only those who had known her for quite a long time could see the gradual changes in behavior indicating that Mrs. Engel was failing. Her speech was unchanged—even in simple amenities her speech remained rapid, clipped, and curiously assertive, every syllable coming sharply formed through her heavy European accent. At the same time, she had become slightly more bent forward, and slightly more cautious in her walk. She took shorter steps than before. Her eyes, dark and quick-glancing, were the same, and so was the way she smiled when she greeted you—a sincere, eager, yet at the same time compressed, almost self-canceling smile. But, over time, she grew eccentric. Before outings, she would put on her lipstick too abundantly, and flecks of bright red took resting places on her front teeth. Her paranoia about germs made her unwilling to touch the elevator door, either to pull it open from the outside or to push it open from the inside. To avoid contamination, she never left her apartment without a wadded tissue to use as protection between her fingers and those surfaces. As time went on, she found even the used tissue to be tainted and would drop it at once after using it. The crumpled pieces on the floor of the elevator car told you that Mrs. Engel had been there, and it grew common to find her in the lobby, fumbling in her purse for a new tissue that would allow her safely to push open the front door from the foyer to the street. She was wholly unembarrassed by these habits, and if you freed her from more tissue-searching by, say, opening the front door so she could go through without touching it, her expressions of gratitude were not only profuse, but repeated sometimes to the point where it almost seemed they might never end.

Because I was taking in Mrs. Engel's mail for her again during what was to be her last summer, I may have gotten an earlier hint than others, though a faint one, that she was falling sick. This hint came in the form of her returning early, in fact more than a week early, from the Brooklyn seaside. She came back, she said, because of the food. She explained this to me in tones that made for a severe criticism of those who prepared the food, but also with an underlying hint of revulsion at the very thought of it. As always, Mrs. Engel stood in the hall outside my door as I handed her the packaged mail and the small key with her signature loop of gray string through its head. The food at the hotel, she confided, had been "terrible, terrible." She puckered her lips and wrinkled her nose. "Terrible," she repeated. It didn't occur to me then, but only later, after I had talked with the super, that Mrs. Engel had begun to give up eating.

The super at that time was Ramón Figueroa. I called him the "Good Ramón," a distinction, as you can guess, from an earlier 'bad' counterpart of the same name. The Good Ramón was short, in his late sixties, overwhelmingly generous, extremely friendly, even jovial. He was a very hard worker, though tenants complained often about dirt in the back stairs and hallways and about smeared glass on the front doors. The trouble in that regard lay with no failure in Ramón's good intentions, but it lay with his eyes: He was perfectly willing to clean up the dirt, but half the time he wasn't able to see it and so didn't know it was there.

He was a wonderful gossip and an even better tease. Of someone universally despised in the management office he would say, "He's gonef. You know gonef?" Or about one tenant or another, he might lean toward me and say in a stage whisper "He's meshuge. You know meshuge?"

Completely unselfconscious, he was a consummate actor, especially hilarious in playing the flirt. The remarkable thing is that he actually did gain the trust of the women he chose to flirt with. One of these was Sandra Jenkins, in her fifties, an academic, and a lesbian who had just recently stopped living with her partner of many years. She insisted firmly to any innocent offenders that she chose to be addressed as "Sandra" rather than "Sandy." But the good Ramón, if she happened to pass by while he was, say, in the lobby talking with other tenants, would put his arm around her and speak his lines, in part to her and in part to everyone. His joviality disarmed even the blazer-and-wool-slacks Sandra. "Sandy!" Ramón would say excitedly. "You're my girlfriend, aren't you, Sandy. I've missed you, Sandy!" And Then to all: "Did you know that Sandy and I are going to get married?"

The Good Ramón also flirted even with Mrs. Engel herself. And I swear—when he put his arm around her waist and said, "Did you know that Mrs. Engel and I are going to get married?"—I swear that more than once I saw Mrs. Engel drop her eyes and smile with an embarrassed sort of coquettish pleasure.

The Good Ramón was a simple enough man, but he was a good one, a bringer of happiness whenever he could manage it, and a man whose generosity of spirit was boundless. He had his own wife, the quiet, shy, seldom-seen Tina, and his flirtations were understood by everyone as nothing more than his own expressions of amusement and camaraderie. But, as with all comedy, there was another side to it as well. Ramón actually did manage to earn Mrs. Engel's trust—and one result was that, of all people in the world, she allowed only him into her apartment. I'm sure that if there had been a flood or fire, rescuers would have forced their way in. But such a thing never happened, and, for the decade that he remained as super, only Ramón had entry. And he kept that fact a secret,

what I will miss most is
running into you in
the elevator or on the street
or in the coffee shop.

A person thinks of old familiar
phrases — then and now, for example.
Life and hope. Past and future.
Hope eternal.

too. Only at the end did he break his trust with Mrs. Engel and let the EMS into her apartment.

It turned out to be true that she had stopped eating. And she no longer left her apartment, but counted on Ramón to bring things to her. Toward the end all she wanted, or all she would take, was seltzer. What could he do? He brought seltzer to Mrs. Engel.

Not long after Mrs. Engel died, Ramón and Tina went back to Puerto Rico, where Ramón had built a house years earlier during one of his home-stays between spells of work in New York City. Our new super was named Francisco Sanchez. He was a shy but well-intended, with a small family of his own. He must have been twenty-five, three entire decades younger than Ramón.

Just as Charlie Vogel's had, Mrs. Engel's apartment remained vacant—silent, empty, undisturbed—but for an even longer time. It stayed that way for almost a full year, from late one summer well into the next. Maybe some perversely tangled legal question was being resolved. I don't know. Then one day two men came, with keys. They opened the door, went in, stayed for some time. They came out again and left the building. Francisco told me about it. I wasn't home and hadn't seen it. Even if I had been at home, I still, in all likelihood, wouldn't have seen it.

A day or two later, amid engine-roar and screeching, a green dumpster was back-loaded off a truck and pushed against the curb in front of our house. The next day, four unshaven men arrived, went into Mrs. Engel's apartment, and set to work. Later, they would go back and forth from the apartment to the dumpster, dragging enormous canvas bags bulging with—things. They wore bandannas pulled tightly over their heads and knotted in back, making these workers look like escapees or villains, characters out of Dickens.

From the time we'd first moved in thirty years earlier, the narrow milk-glass shelf over one of our bathroom sinks had been missing—broken, I suppose, who knows how or how many years back. And the bulb over that same sink was stark and glaring, lacking a shade of the same kind of glass—molded like a sea shell—as the one in the other bathroom.

Mrs. Engel's apartment was in the same line as ours, two floors below. I asked Francisco if I could go in to see whether there might be a shelf and light shade in one of her bathrooms, so as to replace our missing ones. He said, yes, of course. The door was not locked. The men with bandannas were at lunch.

This was the year when Gavin was at home, between dance companies, when she was free-lancing from home as a base. That particular morning, she'd already taken class and come back, so she and I went together on our search for the two glass pieces.

By this time, we were entering the early years—right after 9/11—of what I call The Age of Official Piracy. This, to me, is a desolate period that we're still deeply mired in as of this writing and that we're unlikely to be free of for a considerable time. In the case of our own apartment building, The Age of Official Piracy meant that when a tenant died—or moved out in some more voluntary way—that tenant's apartment would be destroyed.

The outer walls would be left as they were, but various choices of interior walls would be gone at with sledge hammers and crow-bars until they were no longer there, in order to allow a "reconfiguring" to one extent or another of the floor plan. The sledge hammers would be put to use also in breaking up original bathroom fixtures and terrazzo flooring, in order than the sturdy or irreplaceable (like our shelf and lampshade) could be replaced with the less sturdy but "modern." Wall-trim, picture moldings, and baseboards would be stripped away and thrown out so that the look of the interior would be detail-free, while the plaster-over-lath-over-concrete walls that had been demolished would be replaced by aluminum uprights faced with drywall—the kind of structure a person could swing an iron frying pan through. Even the oak and walnut parquet flooring, three-quarters-inch thick and there since 1925 when it was laid in by hand, would be crow-barred up and thrown away, to be replaced by adhesive-backed sheets of thin, factory-made flooring.

Something in America despises the old and wants rid of it by almost any measure. In New York City, regulations were put in place to encourage such demolition. These rules declared that a landlord, if he or she "invested" a certain amount of money in the "renovation" of a vacated apartment, could then rent it not under existing regulatory laws, but under the terms of the "free market." That meant as high as the market would bear.

I include this information for two reasons. The first is to dissuade readers from thinking that my daughter and I were ourselves preying either on Mrs. Engel's apartment or, worse, on Mrs. Engel herself. Her glass shelf and glass light shade, before being taken out through the door of her apartment, would have met with sledge, wrench, or swing of peen if Gavin and I hadn't come to rescue them as we did. (As we had suspected, both pieces of glass were there, in the back bathroom, waiting for us.)

And the second reason for my including this information is to clarify why the things that were about to happen to Mrs. Engel's apartment did happen.

It is eerie to go into an apartment when the person who lives—or lived— there is absent. When the person is absent through having died, it is even more so.

When we pushed the door open and went in, it seemed as if suddenly we were in the midst of the past sixty years and that they were all taking place at once. Compressed by some freakish power, all those years were right there, inside the apartment, all of them existing at the same time.

The floor plan of Mrs. Engel's apartment was the same as ours. From her foyer, you could go into either the kitchen, the dining room, the living room, or down a hall to the bedrooms. The kitchen was around to the left. The dining room was almost straight ahead, and the living room, to the right, could be seen easily from a position just inside the front door. The windows of both rooms were bare, without curtain, sash, or shade, and in neither room was there so much as a single stick of furniture. On the floor in the center of each room, however, there lay a mound of debris seven or eight feet across and, at the midpoint, almost a yard deep.

Three scoop-shovels had been pushed under the edges of the mound in the living room and left there, so that their handles, pointing in different directions, all stood up at the same angle.

I felt as though I shouldn't be where I was. It made no difference that the place had already been changed—the debris shoveled and swept into the center of each room by the workmen, the furniture gone, the windows bared, the shovels left standing. It was still Mrs. Engel's apartment. These were still the very rooms she had lived in for six decades.

By entering the apartment, it was as though I were brutalizing her in some obscure way.

But come in I did, and Gavin with me. We weren't coming in as thieves of property, but possibly we were doing something as bad—coming in as thieves of memory, or maybe as thieves of knowledge.

In the dining room, Gavin and I stood looking at the mound. A street-sweeper's broom, long-handled and brown-bristled, lay on the floor. In a corner by the windows stood a dusty but empty wheelbarrow. Judging by it, and by the shovels in the other room, I understood what was going to happen next.

I looked at the mound more closely. The dominant color was dust-gray, but within it was all manner of material—magazines, both splayed and closed, newspapers, letters, envelopes, receipts, bills and invoices, notices, ads, coins, here and there a dollar bill, pieces of cardboard boxes, labels, crumpled tissues past count, pieces of clothing: A fabric-covered belt, a knee-length nylon stocking, a black high-heeled shoe.

Which way is it, do you think? Is history made out of time? Or is it made out of things?

I don't know the answer. I have no idea, really, when Mrs. Engel may have begun simply dropping things on the floor instead of filing them away in one place or another—how long ago it was when she began dropping the statements of her stock earnings onto the floor of one room or another, for example, or the notices that came addressed to her father, those and all the other items like the ones I had gathered from her mailbox when she was away at the shore in Brooklyn.

I remember Mrs. Engel, each year, calling on the telephone two or three days after her return, asking if she could come up. I always said, yes, of course. And I remember how she would stand in the hallway outside the open door to our apartment, saying to me, "I don't have the words to thank you, Mr. Larsen. I don't have the words to thank you."

I would give her the mailbox key, complete with the loop of string she had tied to it. I would give her the shopping bag of mail I had collected. Then, two or three days later, she would telephone again, appear in the hallway again, and this time she would hand me two bottles of wine, one red and one white, one sweet and one dry.

"I don't have the words to thank you," she would say again, bending forward in her bird-like way, giving me the hint of a bow. In her hands, free now from holding the wine, was the usual white tissue, which she would pluck at absently as she spoke. Her mouth was the usual shockingly bright red. "I don't have the words to thank you," she said, as I tried, in any way I could, to assure her that no thanks were due, that it had been very, very little trouble, that I had, really, not done anything, that I had done nothing for her at all.

2

WHEN MY WIFE AND I MOVED INTO THE BUILDING, as I mentioned before, there were no children in it other than the two Vogel boys, then six and eight or thereabout, and the last of Mrs. Weilberg's three sons, who was then entering junior high school. There was also, it's true, Mrs. Temkin's younger son, Sal, who still lived at home while he went to City College.

As for infants, however, or other children who might be playmates for our own daughters as they grew—not a one. In the whole building, as I said, there wasn't a single family dog. It was, when we moved in, a building either of old-ness or of rapidly approaching oldness. There was the retired Juilliard teacher, Mr. Karel—a bachelor who sported a beret and long cigarette-holder—who was to die in the early 1990s; there were Mr. and Mrs. Kaminsky, who moved to the southwest, for Mr. Kaminsky's lungs, in the mid-1970s; and there were the families who had come to the United States ahead of or during WWII—Mr. and Mrs. Temkin; Mrs. Engel; Mr. and Mrs. Weilberg; and Mr. Ernst, who died in mid-1990s, shortly pre-deceasing the dapper piano teacher, Mr. Karel.

Mr. Ernst moved into the building as a boy, with his parents, in the late 1930s, and for his entire life afterward he lived in exactly the same apartment— on the front of the building on the second floor, overlooking the street. He married very late in life. Whether he had had an earlier marriage, I don't know, but I do know that from 1971 until 1990, he lived alone. When he married then, in 1990, it was to a woman his own age, Miriam, who was of a pronouncedly, extraordinarily sweet temperament. Like Egon Karel, she, too, had been a pianist, but very, very far back. Now, late in life, she suffered from a disease that caused an extreme shaking of her hands and a slight, almost metronome-like nodding of her head. The story of her life was in some ways almost unimaginable. She had already been married, as a young woman, in Germany, and her young husband had been killed by the Nazis. I have no details. I know only that he was killed before the war had actually begun, in fact even before Kristallnacht, in November 1938.

After her husband was murdered, Miriam came to New York—near the same time as Mr. Ernst did, with her parents. Her family settled in an apartment two blocks away, on the same street but closer to the river. The families knew one another, socialized, did things together. And then, after decades and decades had passed, when they were the only two left of all the original people, Miriam and Egon got married.

Miriam doted on her old friend, now her new husband. For many years, from the early 1950s on, Mr. Ernst had run an insurance office in the neighborhood, and he still went in to work almost every day. I myself often came home from classes around four in the afternoon, and as I turned into our street and headed toward our building, I would see Miriam looking out from the window of their apartment that, of all six of its front windows, was the one closest to Broadway. It must be that she sat in a chair pulled up as close to the sill as it could go, because she would be looking down our street toward Broadway and the very corner that I myself had just turned. She paid me no attention, but seemed to be watching only for Mr. Ernst. I was quite near to her as I passed under the window, and I could observe her in considerable detail. Her expression was sweet, patient, innocent—and, or so I imagined, longing. Her head would be nodding very slightly in its metronomic way, and, coming to me through dust-filmed glass panes, her face looked almost imaginary or like something from an antique painting. At such times, I thought of her as a spirit of the building, summoned up from deep time and great distances to sit right there, in that posture, at that window, during all these afternoons. If she really had been married before 1938, her birth could have been in, say, 1920, perhaps even earlier, before the building she now sat in even existed. Like others, she was an attendant spirit of the apartment house, tying it to another side of the world, to terrors it was never to know, to a time so distant that, if care weren't taken, it risked being lost altogether.

3

OTHERS ARRIVED, SOME TO REMAIN BRIEFLY, some to stay on. Many died. An opera singer came to one of the back apartments on the ground floor, and from eight or nine floors above, on the rare occasions when the windows were open, you could hear her practicing. She married an anesthesiologist and they moved away. A very beautiful and athletic young woman, on the fourth floor, had an accident while skiing and within a second's time was destined to life in a wheelchair. She remained beautiful, and also inexplicably cheerful as her more taciturn—and handsome—young husband pushed and maneuvered her chair wherever they went. Before long, they also moved away. In later years, after the millennium came and went, others replaced them, mostly younger couples in the professions or finance, many with young children.

It was as though the mood and character of the building had changed only very slowly for several decades, and then, suddenly, at century's end, sped up enormously. I think that the same thing was true also of the nation. The mood and character of the entire nation had changed bit by bit for perhaps a decade and a half, and then suddenly, halfway or so through the 1990s, everything sped up greatly.

When the year 2000 came and went, and when the change in pace of the sort we're talking about took place, something else of tremendous importance happened. That important thing was that the past itself, all at once, fell drastically in value.

It fell in value so greatly, in fact, that eliminating the past altogether came to be considered by a great many thinkers, merchants, dealers, protesters, landlords, legislators, bankers, and politicians as the most useful and profitable thing that could and should be done with it.

This is part of the reason why, when apartments became vacant, workmen moved in—the way they did into Mrs. Engel's apartment—and peeled, hammered, stripped, eliminated, and broke off every vestige of the past they could, until the dwelling no longer looked like the inside of a building built in 1925, but like the inside of a building put up in 1998, or 2003, or 2010. The aim was to remove the record of time, to remove even the presence of time—of history—itself, and to transform each apartment into something smooth, sharp-edged, trim, white, modern, undetailed, and without idiosyncrasy.

Along with this surgical scraping-out of the apartments, there would be also a concomitant scraping-out of the remnants, ghosts, and presences of those who had lived in the apartments before. Like the nation, the building we live in is having its past taken away from it. It is undergoing a putatively

mandatory surgery that, to my own way of thinking, removes something not
only invaluable but something that, once gone, cannot be retrieved by any
power known to humankind.

It's natural to wonder who lived in the building eighty-five years back,
when it was newly built and the neighborhood was burgeoning. Those people
would have been a mixture—Irish, certainly, Italian, many varieties of Ameri-
cans—people by and large doing quite well for themselves as merchants, import-
ers, wholesalers, distributors, now and then professionals—as in law, for example.
When 1937 and 1938 came along, things changed, as we have seen. Many of those
first tenants (at least some of whom must actually have had live-in maids to stay
in the tiny rooms intended for them in the larger apartments, with their miniature
quarter-baths), those first tenants, I don't doubt, moved to Long Island, West-
chester, and northern New Jersey as others came to replace them, families like the
Ernsts, for example, in insurance brokerage, or the Temkins and Weilbergs—
diamond cutters, both—or the Engel family, the family of Rabbi Engel.

The years not stopping, always going by. Mrs. Engel moving in, with her
father and perhaps her mother, in the year of my own birth, 1941, when not
only was there a doorman but, if Mrs. Engel was right, one who wore white
gloves. The Weilbergs arrived in 1946, immediately after the end of the war. The
Temkins didn't come until 1962, although they lived in the immediate neighborhood, under much more penurious circumstances, from 1944 until their move
to the apartment house. Sal, the elder of the Temkin sons, told me what a joy it
was for his brother and him, in the comparatively large new apartment, to have
a *bedroom*.

The building saw everything and it heard everything as well. As we ponder
its watching and listening, the same question from earlier comes back again,
though in a slightly different form: Is time made up of the things that happen
during it, or is time made up of the objects that exist inside of it? Are museums
collections of time, or are they collections of objects? On the front of our apartment building is a museum-object, so familiar that it goes unseen—the small
iron box, painted thickly in ancient coats of red: The watchman's clock-point on
his neighborhood rounds during World War II. And, from a decade or so later,
during the mix of blandness and utter terror that comprised the 1950s, there
hangs on the front of the building a weathered yellow-and-black Civil Defense
sign, the size of a dinner plate, painted with the radiation symbol and the words
"Fallout Shelter."

In reality there is no shelter from anything, at least not in one way of
thinking. Everything begins, continues, ends, although some things take longer

to do so than others. The apartment house will end, too, someday. But in the meantime it will continue to house every person who ever lived in it, harbor every event that ever took place in it, and be the container for the spirit of every object that ever existed in it.

1960, 1965, 1970, 1975. There was the super, who lived in the basement, who kept a Great Dane and carried a long-sword when he was called to look into trouble. There was the gay couple, one of whom committed suicide, no one ever knowing why, his bereft partner moving away very soon afterward. There was the well-known writer who lost his son to an accident and then fell into a downward spiral of grief that took him to his own end. Still, no one from the building died in the Vietnam war, although a slashing in the elevator was terrifying and bloody but not critical. Drugs were everywhere across the Upper West Side. One evening, two burglars swinging up from a hallway window into a kitchen half a floor above, breaking the window-glass and wriggling in head first with nothing but nine floors of air below them and a concrete slab to land on. One of the two never to be seen again, the other snagged by the cops on his way out through the front door with a television set in his arms. Or the afternoon when Sal Temkin, coming home from classes at CCNY, surprised a burglar in the back rooms of his family's apartment. Sal screaming at him, the guy fleeing out the back kitchen door and down the stairs, Sal after him—when the burglar dropped the gallon-size pickle-jar full of dimes, nickels, quarters, and halves, making a sound that cascaded across three flights of uncarpeted cement stairs like the world coming to an end.

The house of life, the house of mirth, the house of grief, the house of joy. So many people now gone, the year having rolled around to 2010, and at the same time so many new people having arrived. There are kids all over the place now, no fewer than three more very soon to be born, and by my count three pet dogs in residence plus a fourth that visits frequently.

That long-ago afternoon when Gavin and I went into Mrs. Engel's vacant apartment. Finding that she had slept in the smaller of the two bedrooms, not the one that might once have been the rabbi's—and that in the smaller room was a set of twin beds. Could Mrs. Engel ever, conceivably, have had a sister? And, if so, what could possibly have happened to her?

I have no way of knowing. It is too late now. There is no one left to ask.

The workmen had not yet shoveled or swept the floor of Mrs. Engel's bedroom. The unwashed windows were so grimy as to let in only diminished light. Twin bureau-tops stood obscured in half-darkness under mounds of clothing, decades'-worth of garments tossed one atop another. The upper part of a white silk slip hung down, backwards, its dangling straps suggesting the arms of someone who had flung herself backward, how many years before, and had been falling ever since.

Mrs. Engel had chosen for her own bed the one farther away from the windows. In fact, it had been drawn across the room and up against the inner wall, as close to the interior of the apartment as possible. Night, week, month, year, decade, decade, decade, Mrs. Engel slept there, so often, so many times, that the bed was no longer recognizable as a piece of furniture so much as a kind of human nest. The head and foot of the bed were still there, and the boards along the sides. But the bed itself, the mattress and the springs under it, hung down in the concave shape of a swallow's nest, resting on the floor.

On our way out through the foyer, I drew open the door of the coat-closet there. Inside, the same as in our own foyer closet, was a wide wooden shelf running from one side to the other, above the clothes-pole. On that shelf stood twelve or fifteen books, upright, spines out. They were identical, in white wrappers, the lettering in bright blue.

I reached up for one and opened it. It was a volume of poetry, in Yiddish, impossible for me to read. I reversed the book, opened it from left to right, went past the first title page and on to a second one: The second one had English on it. It was a book by Mrs. Engel, published in 1958. The Yiddish title, transcribed into the Roman alphabet was:

Oygen Reiden and the translation into English: *Eyes Have Spoken*

Then, on the page past the second title page, was a picture of a dark-haired youngish woman whom I couldn't imagine I had ever seen before in my life. She was pretty, with an oval face, her very full hair parted down the center, and something mysterious about the lips and eyes: It was Mrs. Engel, at—what? twenty-eight years of age? thirty-two? thirty-five?

Here was the photo of a person I had never seen before in my life, and yet here also was the photo of a woman I had known fairly well—a woman who had died, whose bedroom I had just visited, whose loneliness through all those three or more long, slow, closing decades of her life, it seemed to me now, suddenly, must have been so empty as to have been insurmountable, immeasurable, unimaginable.

But what could I have done about it, about any of it? What could I possibly have done?

Impulsively, I took the copy of Mrs. Engel's book with me, and Gavin and I left the apartment. I felt like a thief.

Over the following days and weeks, the sounds of demolition—sledging, banging, crashing, wrenching sounds—came up and in through our windows, reverberating also through our floors and walls. The green dumpster at the curb became gradually more and more full. The workmen pushed their wheelbarrows back and forth, with load after load of debris scooped up from the floors of Mrs. Engel's apartment. Then came the contents of the bedroom, the clothing first, tossed haphazardly into the dumpster, where it lay inert, like slain or broken people entangled with one another. After that, the little bit of furniture: The two bureaus, their drawers first, broken down, then the rest, pieces of broken lumber varnished on one side and plain on the other. As the days passed, still more things came out of the apartment. A bathroom sink, then another, absurdly white in the sunshine. Mrs. Engel's tub. A toilet, embarrassing, a gaping thing not to be seen in public. After it, a lid and seat tossed onto the pile. Then another toilet after it, another lid and another seat. A worker climbed up into the dumpster and with a sledge hammer set about breaking up the white ceramic pieces in order to economize on space.

More. Brilliant glint of sunlight in a mirror. And another brilliant glint. Then, in a seemingly endless stream, strips and slats of broken wood—skinny pieces of molding from the walls, the very baseboards, ripped away and broken into manageable lengths, tossed onto the pile to make their own archaeological layer in the dumpster. The very floors themselves came out, slats, strips, broken parquet-pieces of hardwood, more and more of them until they formed their own unbroken and mounded layer, bringing the dumpster up to full.

The sun-filled morning when they pulled the dumpster away, I looked out the window as two workers were starting to pull a tarp over the load from back to front. It turned out that someone else, not only my daughter and I, had looked inside Mrs. Engel's foyer closet. For there, on the very top of the load, Mrs. Engel's dozen or so copies of *Oygen Reiden* had been flung, the last item to be taken from the apartment, an afterthought. The books had come to rest in a perfect curved arc, one volume just overlapping another. Their blue-on-white covers were vivid and stark in the sunlight. Then the workers pulled the tarp across the load and set about the quick business of lashing it down for the trip to landfill. ∎

I don't know how much
longer we're going to be
able to stay here

THE TENANTS

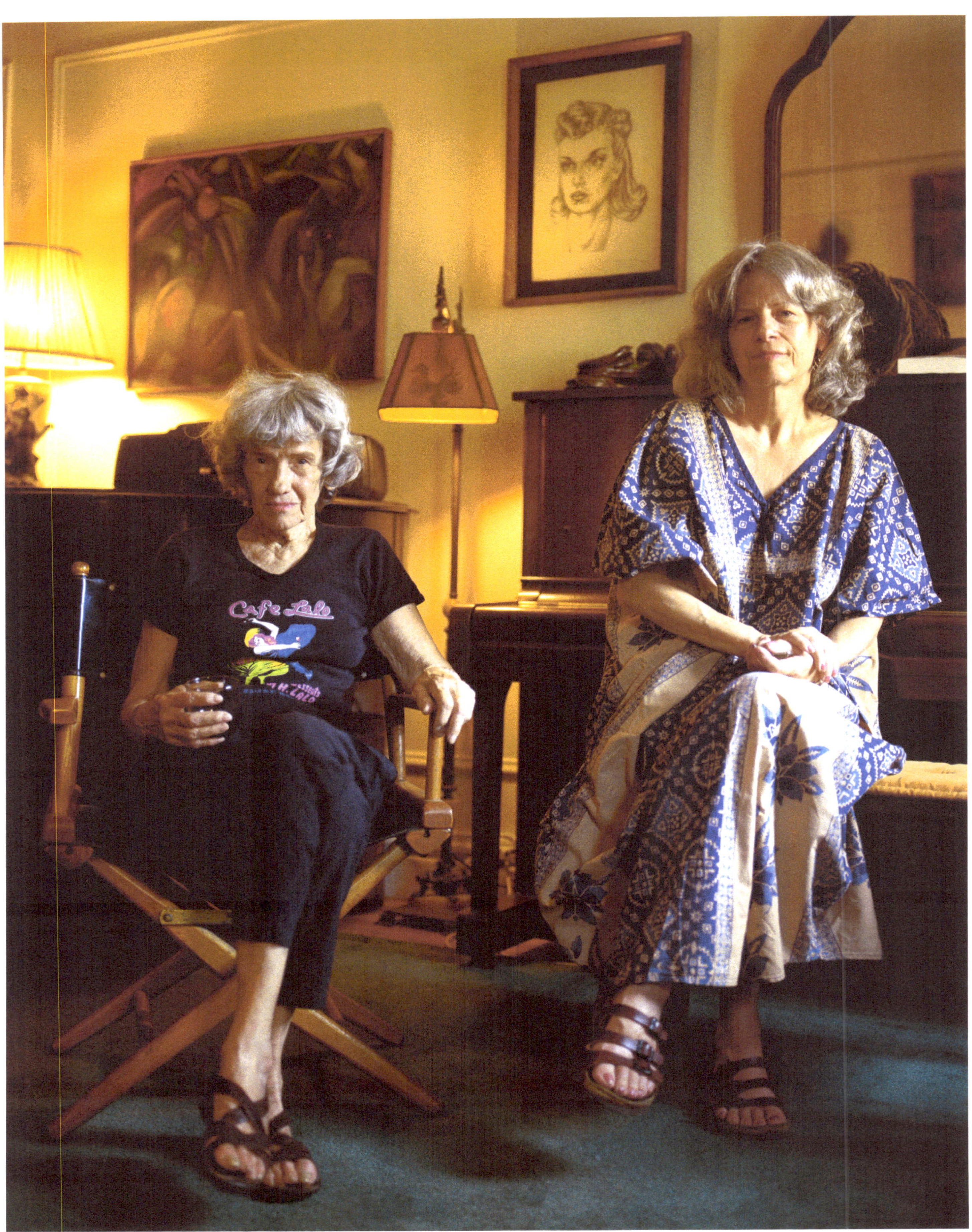

GABY AND LIZ

In 1962, Liz moved into a rear apartment on a low floor with her daughter Gaby, who was then a student at CCNY. Next door lived a family whose son suffered from cerebral palsy and who had suffered hearing loss. In the evenings, the family played the television so loudly that Gaby couldn't concentrate on her studying. "But he can't hear it if it's lower," said the boy's mother. Gaby went to the back of her own apartment, lined the bathtub with pillows, and made herself comfortable. She earned much of her BA from the tub.

When she was baby-sitting for someone in a front apartment on a higher floor, Gaby learned that that family was leaving and asked the landlord whether she and her mother could move upstairs. The deal was done with a nod and handshake, and Liz and Gaby have been in their larger place ever since—lined now with walls of books, graced by three housecats, and filled with decades of memorabilia that speak of the past and of home.

There were no common mailboxes back then, and the super would leave people's mail outside the door of each apartment. Slow but friendly, the super lived in the basement with a Great Dane. When summoned for emergencies, like the wall-bending party thrown by a gay couple on the second floor, he would appear with the enormous dog as sidekick and also with a long sword—that no one ever saw used.

One partner of the gay couple later committed suicide, though whether inside the apartment or out, no one knows. It was very long ago. Back then, says Gaby, each family's apartment "felt like home." But ever since she and her mother were recently lied to by management—instructed to "ignore" an eviction notice that was all too real—there's been a sea-change. After their near-eviction through trickery, the apartment has changed. It doesn't feel like home any more.

Gentrified gradually over the decades, the neighborhood has grown safer while management has grown more dangerous. Rents are going up, laws have changed to let them rise more rapidly, and property owners, scenting blood, are greedy for more.

All their lives, Liz and Gaby have been left wingers. But now things are changing around them. Gaby gives a wistful sigh and says, "I don't know how much longer we're going to be able to stay here."

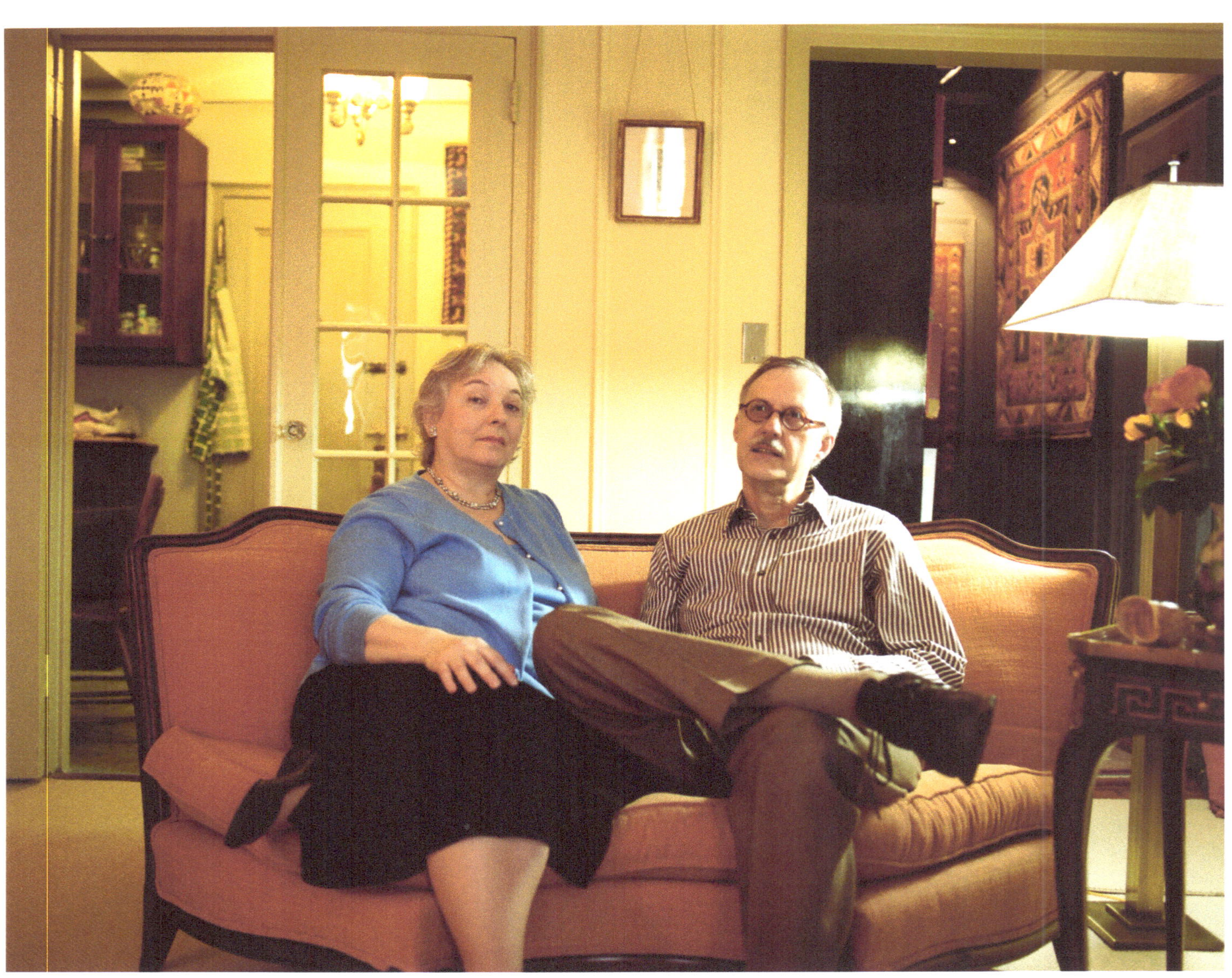

PAUL & CARLOTTA

In 1965, when he came to New York from Mississippi knowing "not a soul," Paul had $400. The money lasted him two months as he looked for work and stayed in the Washington Jefferson Hotel. Once he'd found a job, at least temporarily, a tip led him to apartment 1A, where he roomed with someone already there. Two years later, the roommate gone, the super and Paul traded places, and Paul moved up to the fifth floor after first living in the basement for two weeks while renovations took place.

He enrolled as a doctoral candidate in political science, and, even though he was living on more of a shoe-string than ever, he managed to see the opera or ballet now and then. One night in the recently opened New York State Theater, he sat next to a young woman who was remarkably knowledgeable about ballet. And so it was that Carlotta and Paul met, one night in the middle 1960s, in the last row of the fourth ring, at *Dances at a Gathering* and Antony *Tudor's Dim Luster*.

Carlotta (with a doctorate of her own, in anthropology), spent the early part of her professional life in the study of human movement and dance notation, and now is a major director in arts administration. After his Ph.D., Paul started a successful polling company. He has now retired to a second career as photographer, traveler, and collector.

In the late sixties and early seventies, many tenants in the building were still couples—or widows—who had escaped from Europe during the Nazi era. One such neighbor, widowed, aging, and preparing to move in with relatives, asked Carlotta if she and Paul would like a sofa. The piece had come with her, she said, "from the old world." Her price was $15. This is the sofa that Carlotta and Paul are sitting on in their portrait.

Who knows where in Europe it originated, or when it came into its first owner's possession? Paul and Carlotta themselves have had it now it for forty-one years.

"If this sofa could talk," someone said. It's true: History threads its way through objects just as it does through lives.

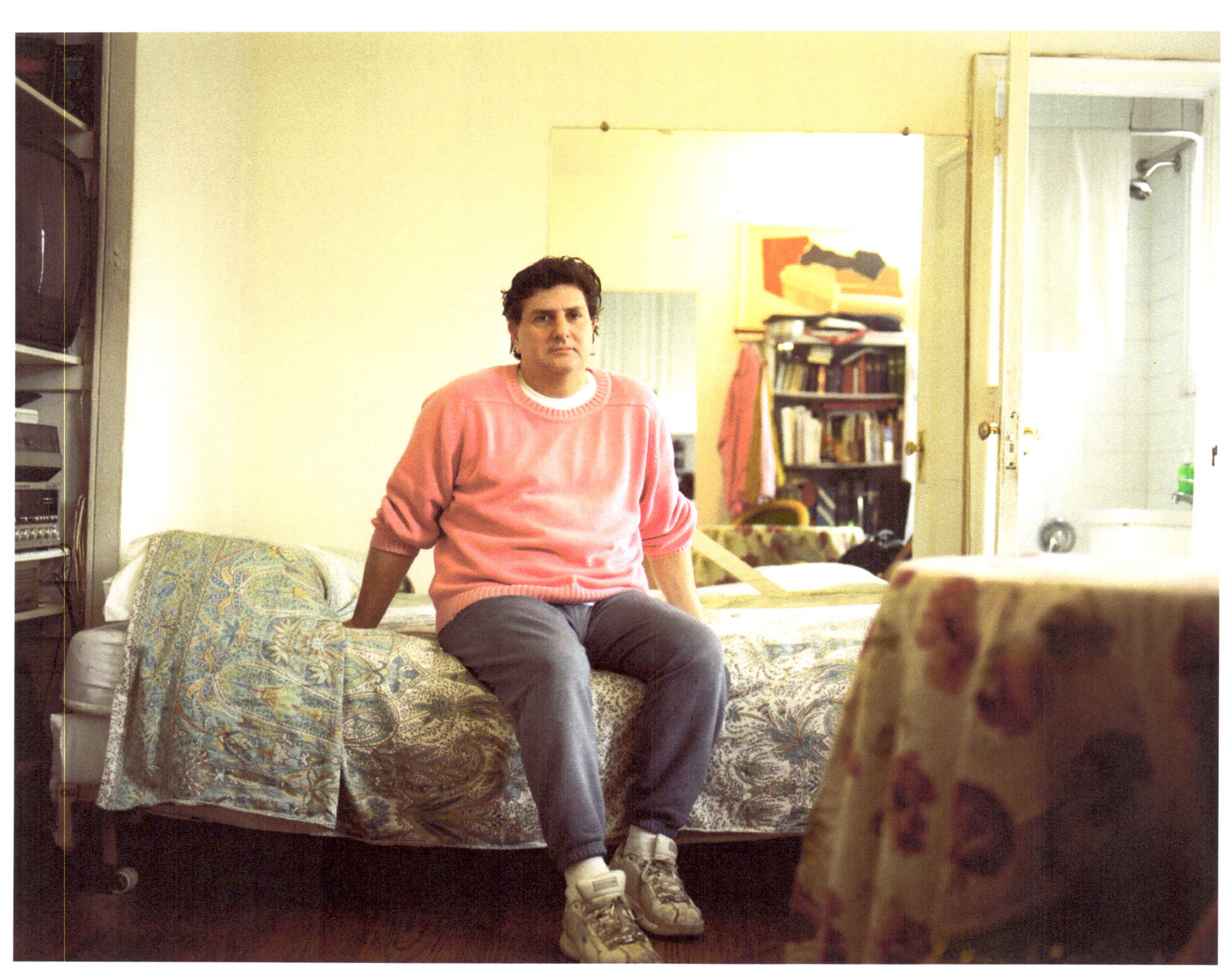

Two blocks away,
a Spanish-style church spire
rises up, looking
surprisingly near.

ADRIANO

Adriano grew up in northern Italy, not far from Lake Como, where his mother still lives. By the time he came to New York, in the late 1980s, he had studied with a number of world-renowned photographers and was a working photographer himself. Even with national and international clients, though, he continued living in a fourth-floor East Village walk-up. When money came, it could be like a banquet. But the feasts were often far apart.

A man of many talents, Adriano filled the lean stretches by working as a waiter, then as a maître d.' Still later, when assignments were increasing and he needed a more flexible schedule, he used his oenophile's talent to become a wine-consultant and provisioner to restaurateurs. Adriano is also a spiritual man. After a ten-year course in the Testaments and theological history, he received his ordination.

In the middle 1990s, he rented the building's smallest penthouse apartment because, though it wasn't even as big as his place in the Village, the owner gave him use of the roof, an open and expansive area. But management has lately begun trying to renege on the agreement—in an attempt, Adriano thinks, to force him out in order to get higher rent. "Money is their god and they stamp on anything for money," he says. He speaks both in sorrow and anger.

His apartment is filled with light, but for the time being—maybe forever—outdoors is only a terrace barely wide enough for a single chair. The cramped space is bounded on its open side by a white iron rail. Two blocks away, a Spanish-style church spire rises up, looking surprisingly near.

He misses the roof, Adriano admits. But, he adds, there's still this little postage stamp of a terrace. In warm weather, he says, when he plays opera in his bedroom but with the door standing open, birds of various kinds circle around and perch on the rail, looking in and listening to the music with him. "I kid you not," he insists. And, given the absolutely serious expression on Adriano's open and guileless face—well, a person believes him.

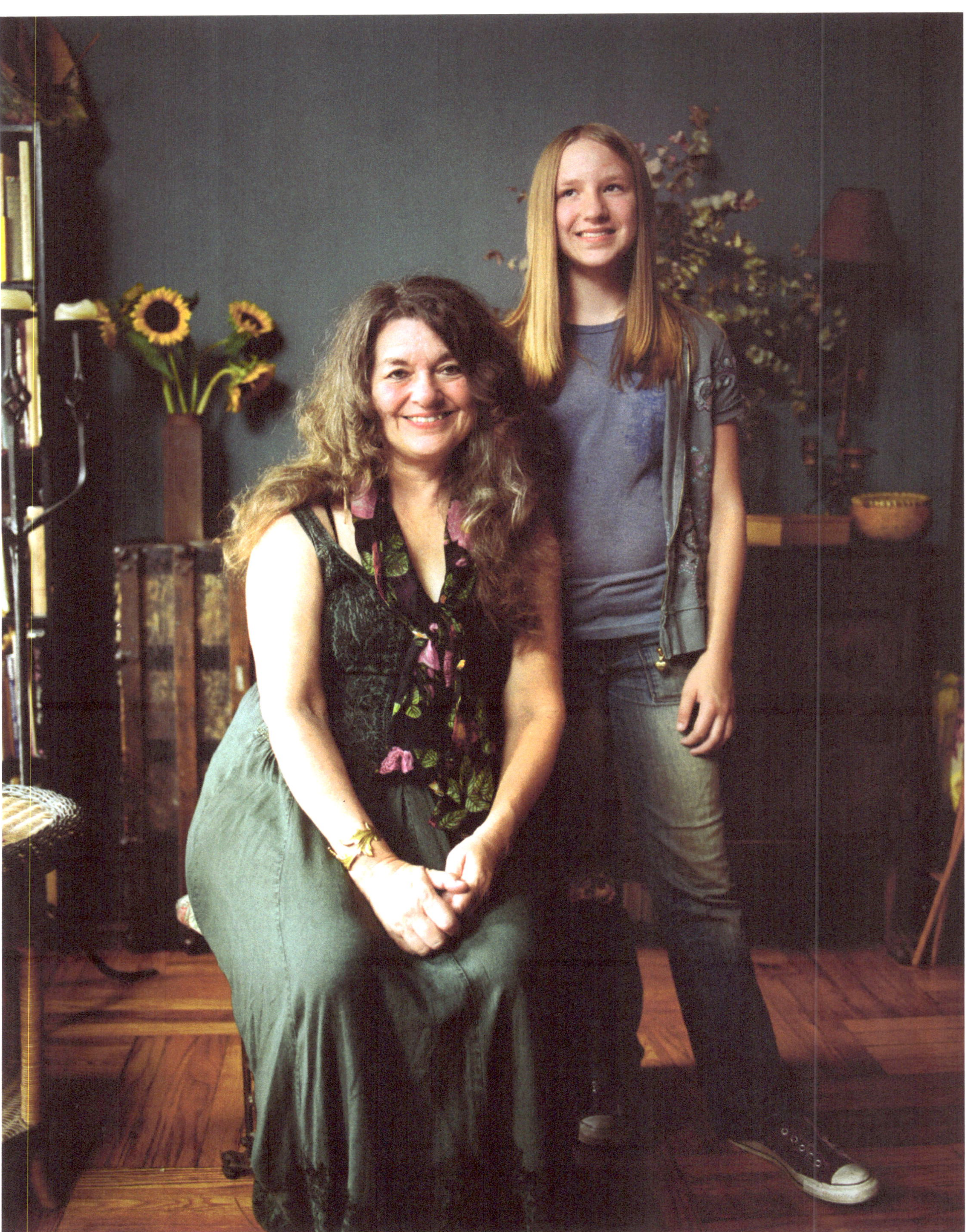

LINDA & HALLIE

Growing up in a small town in the Middle West, Linda never thought she was especially good at music. She did take piano for five years beginning at age seven, and flute lessons later opened the door to the last seat in the high school band. She liked marching in the band because it took place outdoors, but after a time she stopped practicing the instrument and soon after dropped out.

Then one summer a cousin came with his guitar—and of course he let Linda have a go. This was something entirely different. Maybe it was the look of it, the feel, the sound—in any case, Linda took to it and learned chord after chord. She had more music in her than she'd ever imagined.

One day a package dangled from the mailbox by the road—the guitar Linda and her sister Cindy had sent for. One of them would sing and one accompany. Two ukuleles entered the scene. Then a second guitar. And of course all along there was the piano.

Linda majored in speech and theater, and the day after graduation, in 1973, left for New York. Her early days in the city had their frights. An ad led her to a share—in the same apartment as the one in the portrait here. The walls were jet black, the lease so old the name was unknown to anyone, and drawers were filled with strange and bizarre possessions—as if they belonged to a dead man. The dead man himself appeared one night—and then left, taking with him beds, tables, lamps, every last stick of furniture. In the apartment next door there happened to live a quiet young man. When it was dark, he would sometimes rage from his window, hurling obscenities and curses out into the dead of night and the hushed, small hours of the morning.

Once in lower midtown, Linda heard a man's steps behind her. She turned uptown, and the steps were still there. Growing frightened, she turned west; uptown once more; then east—the same steps, still there. The dead man on the lease, the screamer, and now this. Feeling panic, Linda ran up the steps into the Teddy Roosevelt house on 20th Street. She could hide in there. She remained for some time. When she came out, there was no stalker waiting—and she'd been hired as a singer and performer for the National Park Service.

Still in the same apartment, Linda has sung, played, and performed now for thirty-five years. Her daughter is almost out of high school. Inheritor of her mother's talent, she plays trumpet, piano, violin, ukulele—and guitar.

If you were to think
of a building's tenants as
representing elements
of its pyschology, Maureen
would be this building's
conscience.

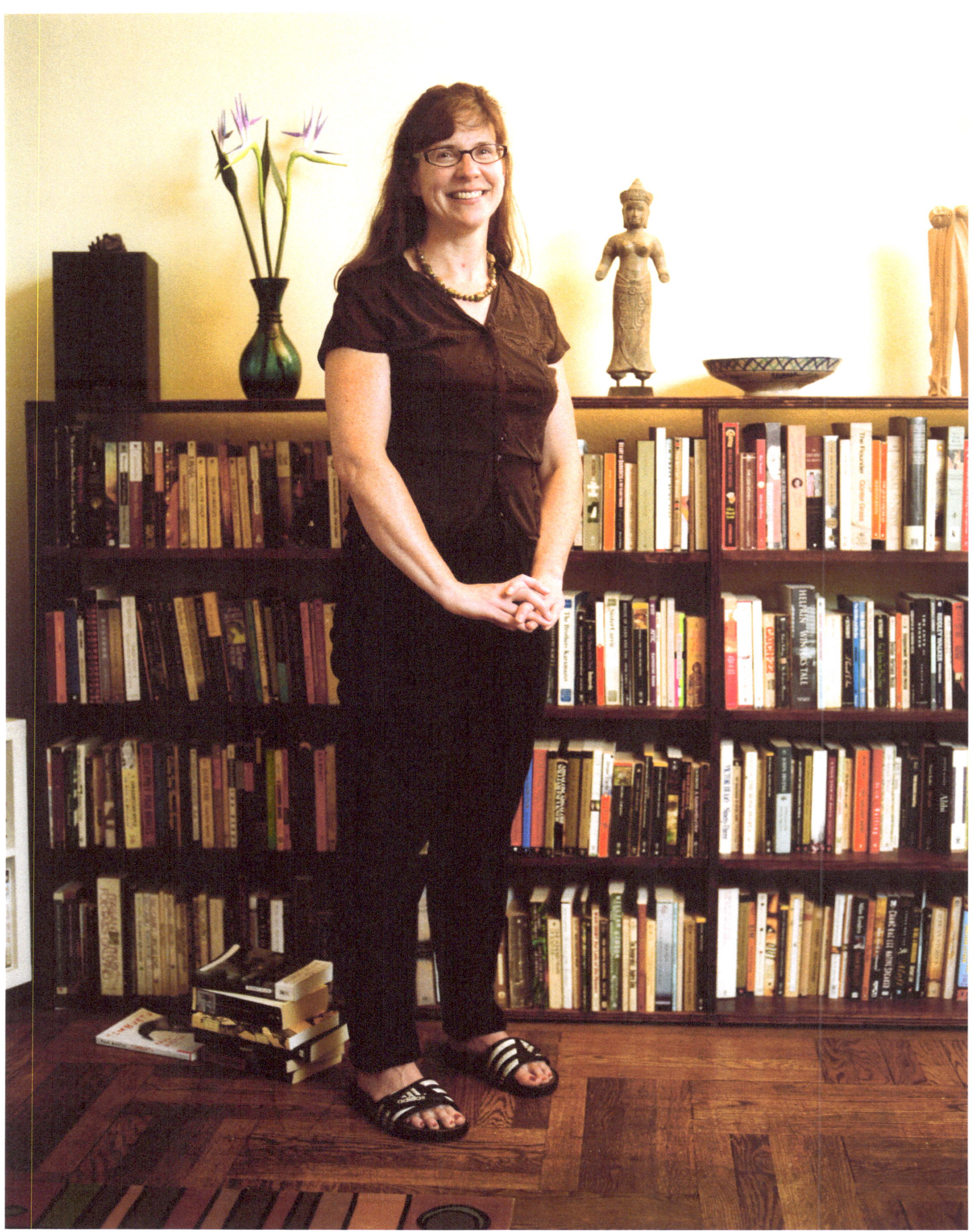

MAUREEN

If you were to think of a building's tenants as representing elements of its psychology, Maureen would be this building's conscience. Maureen, after all, has dedicated her professional life to the amelioration, ideally to the avoiding altogether, of suffering in others.

However serious, this conscience is also an upbeat, wholesome, affirming one. When she was young, says Maureen, she was a "bad girl." In adulthood, nevertheless, she holds a doctorate in epidemiology, with a specialty in AIDS research, and, as she'll tell you, a memory of having "cried all the way through her dissertation."

The "bad" part? Maureen wanted to have a "good time," and that meant traveling—through Central and South America, most of Europe, a lot of Africa, through much if not most of southeast Asia, and more. Between her journeys, she would enroll in one college after another—and then leave one college after another, sans degree, to go off to other parts of the world.

Then came the change, when she saw friends dying at impossibly young ages. She moved to this building because her sister lived there. When her sister married and went off elsewhere, Maureen stayed. She went for her bachelor's and stuck with it (she even married her Spanish teacher, a wonderful bond that lasted—and then dissolved). On to graduate school, then to the doctorate that grew out of years of research in the plague-beset streets of Brownsville, where the tears fell.

Support for new projects came from the National Science Foundation— then withered away with the political sea-change after 2000. Maureen teaches now at an upstate medical college, but, as she says, the school is "imploding" and she doubts there's a future there, just as she doubts future support for meaningful research.

When she first moved in, she remembers, she would hear musicians all around—a horn quartet that practiced regularly, a flutist nearby, even the sounds of Gary's baritone voice from upstairs, before he retired. Now, she says, there's not much to hear. It's a bit like friends who have disappeared.

I love my apartment, she says when asked, the customary brightness lighting up in her intelligent eyes. A tri-athlete already, she might have to take up a musical instrument herself, she says. Her words are accompanied by the impromptu lilt of her usual mellifluous laughter.

Ah, for a world of Maureens!

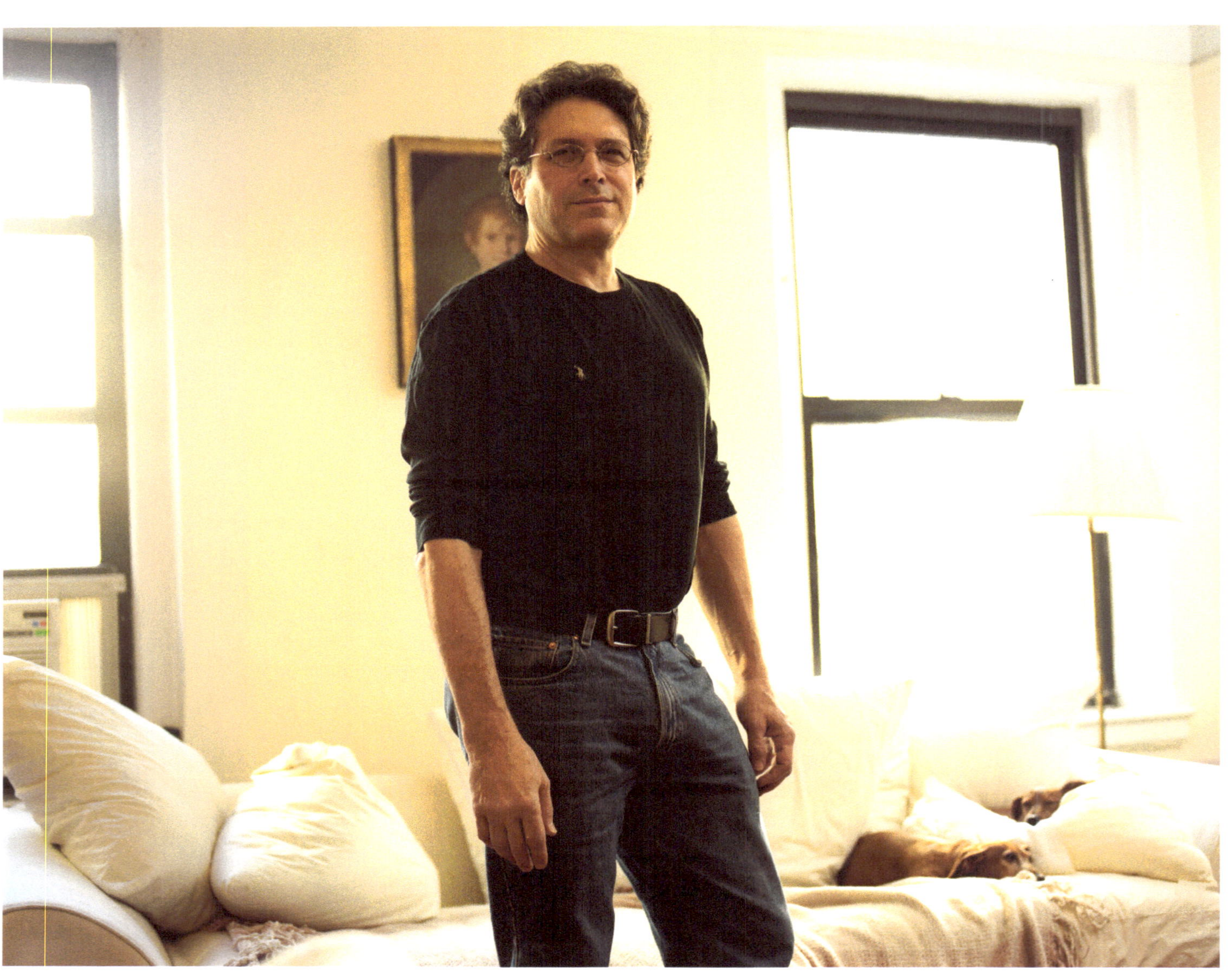

MAX

In 2007, at a point of change in his life, Max moved into the building. In under two years, he had already left for a place elsewhere in the city. Max is younger in appearance than in years. He was for a long time a working journalist, and he is an accomplished poet as well. Now a professional writer, he has a contract for and is researching a major book of non-fiction. He is much missed by tenants still in the building, who came to know him as pleasant, soft-spoken, ever considerate, and as a person always ready for, and most adept at, conversation.

Life brings change, and among the changes for Max when he moved in, besides a switch in profession, were a marriage moving toward its sunset just at the same time as his children were springing off into adulthood. Max enjoyed his fellow tenants more than he did the building itself, which in fact brought him little joy. After moving, he wrote back saying as much:

But, of course, what I will miss most is running into you in the elevator or on the street or Anna in the coffee shop, and I'll miss many of the other people in the building who have been so warm-spirited. I, of course, have no nostalgia, and never will, about the building itself. I will not miss toilets that don't flush 75% of the time if there's anything but piss in the pot; the filthy laundry room, where it sometimes feels as if you're bringing your clothes to add dirt and bacteria, not the other way around; the metal elevator ceiling flapping overhead; or the elevator porthole of double glass with hair and skin cells rising grayly week by week between the panes, an ancient potpourri of DNA. Nor will I miss the lobby with its warm, welcoming feeling, its fine leather couch, and its curtainless window looking out into the garbage next door.

No, I don't think it's a sign of the times that I'm moving out. Only that it seemed insane of me to stay and pay the high rent I was paying while feeling as if someone were stealing money from me each month. There have always been bad landlords just as there have always been cockroaches.

As ever,
Max

And so adieu to Max, with a nod of gratitude—and a droll smile for his poet's sharp eye in making vivid the nature of the house, and of the world, that we many humans dwell in.

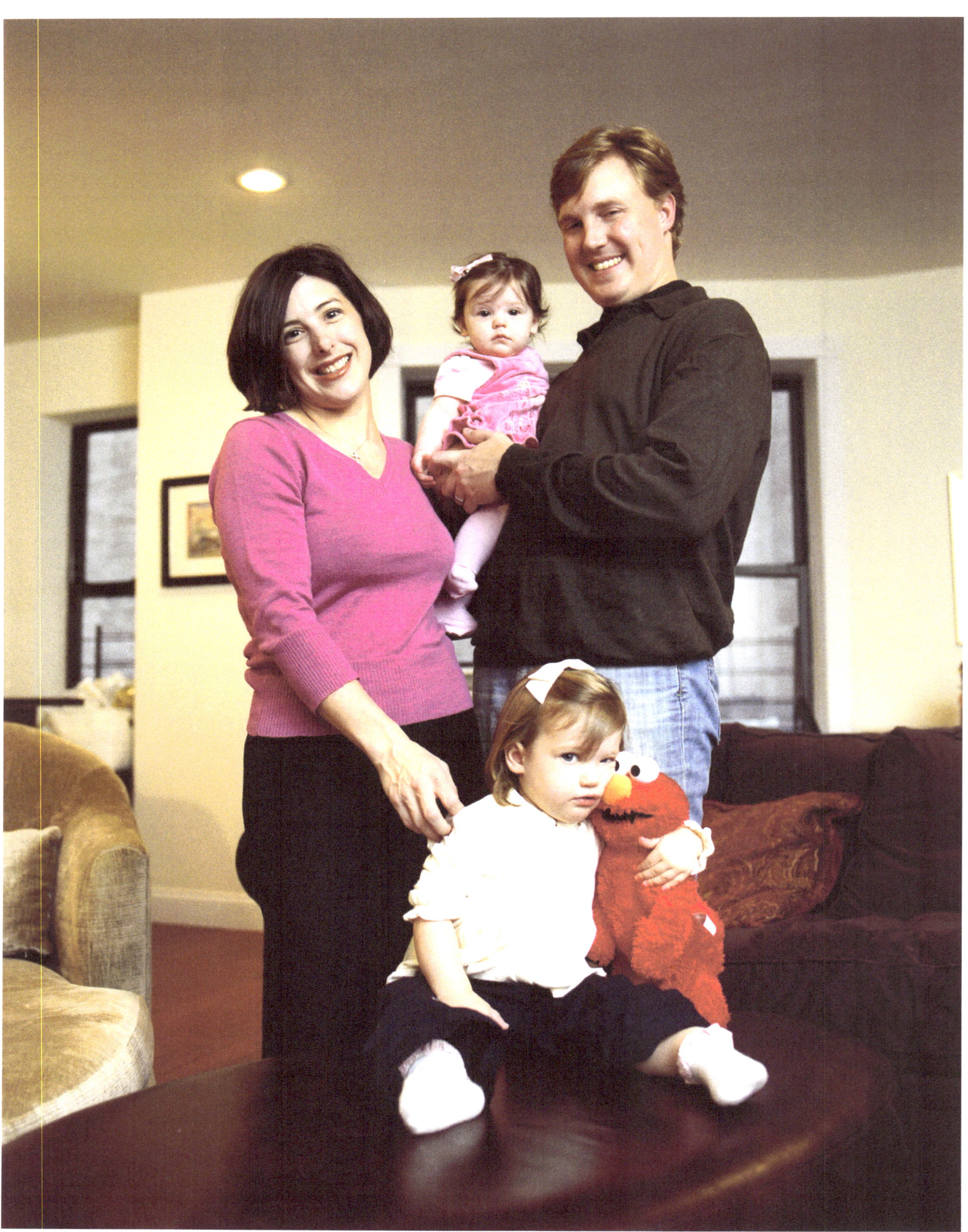

SASHA, TOM, BELLA, & EVIE

If walls could talk, especially the walls in this apartment, they would tell a story of awful drama and great contrast. It would be a story about decades of fear, uncertainty, and sorrow—these now set aside at last and replaced by new lives filled with at least every appearance of plain and simple happiness.

Home now to Sasha and Tom—along with their Bella and little Evie—this is the apartment where Charlie Vogel and his wife Damara lived and raised their sons Topher and Nate—until divorce came, inevitably, and everyone disappeared into the wings except for Charlie, left to face a couple of solitary decades filled with his demons fierce, tragic, and grim.

Nowadays, visitors are constant at Tom and Sasha's place. Little kids get dropped off, mothers stop by to spend an hour or two with the tireless, unfailingly cheerful Sasha, and on weekends a fair crowd of young parents, mothers and fathers both, gathers with their kids for a brunch with tall people standing around amid great numbers of short ones.

Laughter flows into the hallway, as do the sounds of play—through the same door that once failed to muffle sounds of rage and anguish, screams of fear, the crash of plates and glassware flung against walls.

A person thinks of old familiar phrases—like, for example, the phrase history and time, or for better or for worse. Then and now. Life and hope. Past and future. Hope eternal.

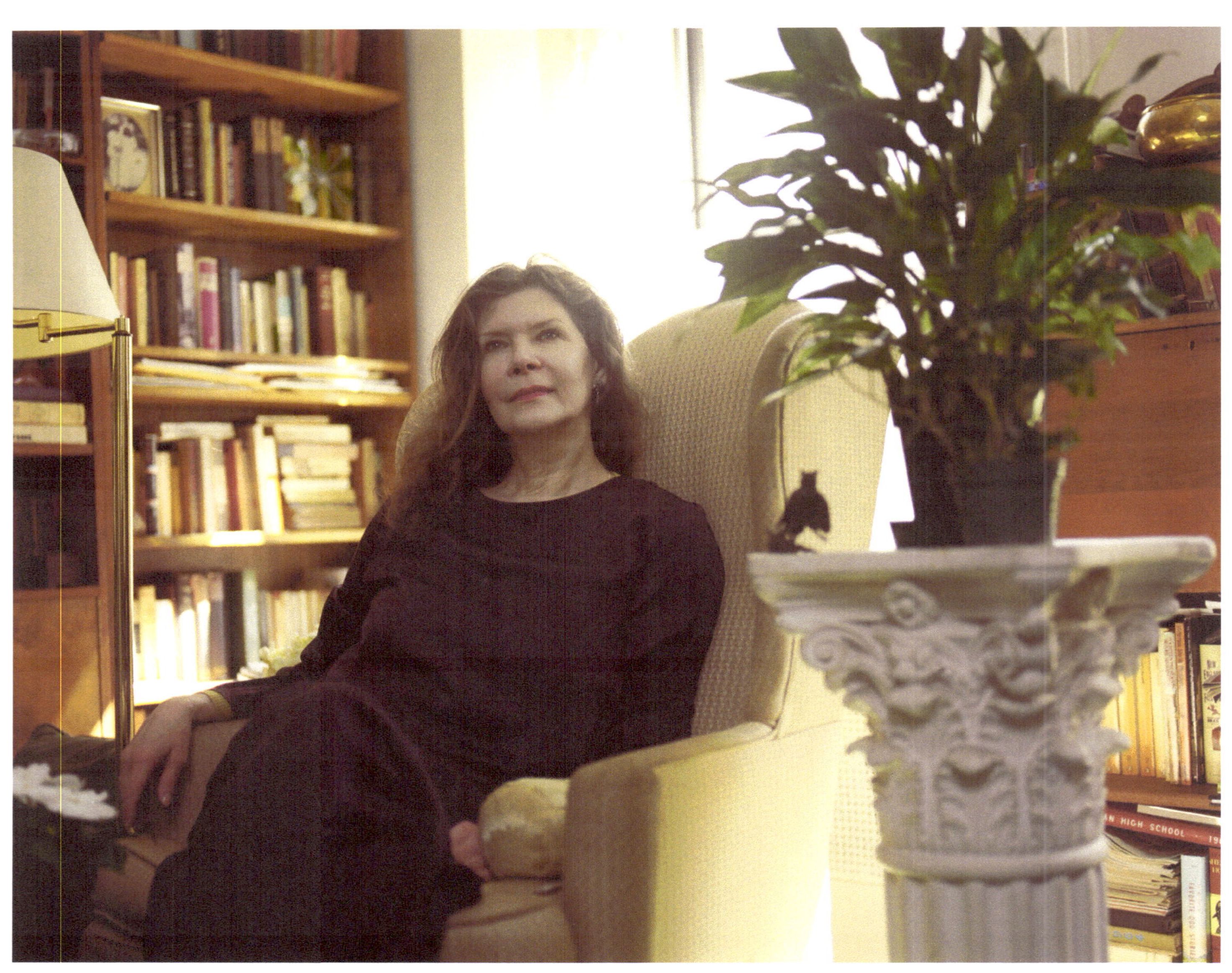

There's a bit of the Celtic in her,
the Arthurian, even something
of the Druidic and the deep, deep,
green faerie past.

GAYLE

Retired from a career as stage actress, Gayle is from two parts of the country. Her mother was—imagine it—a member of the U. S. Marine Corps in WWII. At first, that meant being an airplane mechanic. Later, it meant being assigned as an ambulance driver in Los Angeles, with the job of transporting wounded from incoming ships to military hospitals.

It can't have been easy duty, but it explains how Gayle could have been conceived and born in Los Angeles. Soon after the war, her parents moved to Rhode Island, where Gayle grew up. In the early 1970s, after college, she came to New York, to this apartment, and to life in the theater.

Greatly flexible in the roles she played, Gayle herself is closer to—well— the Deep Romantic. There's a bit of the Celtic in her, the Arthurian, even something of the mysteries, moods, and forested imagery of the Druidic and the deep, green, faerie past.

Her apartment reflects these qualities with its ivied plants and forest-greenery, and with its many icons, images, totems, statues, and sculptures of creatures and objects from nature, including many statuettes of the owl—that being the first word, "owl," her daughter, now grown up and a successful photographer—spoke.

One night, Gayle's next-door neighbor came home and smelled gas. Con Edison had shut off the building's supply for repairs and had failed to restart Gayle's pilot light. The neighbor rang, knocked, called out—but Gayle was asleep in the back room, door closed, slumbering amid shadow, moss, and midsummer magic.

The neighbor called 911. Firemen arrived, pounded at the door—then broke it in. Gayle heard a far-off sound—thunder? She dozed again. Then she awoke to find herself in an immense forest, surrounded by enormous trees reaching to the sky, some of them with lights that darted around, aiming now up to the heavens, now to other trees, now down to the ground.

But these—as Gayle then saw, rising upright on her bed—weren't trees at all. They were firemen, with flashlights. She gazed at them. They gazed at her. Then the play of magic was over.

They were, she said later, very, very kind. And some, she admitted, in her wonderful, breathy voice, were also extremely handsome.

And there they are,
to this day.

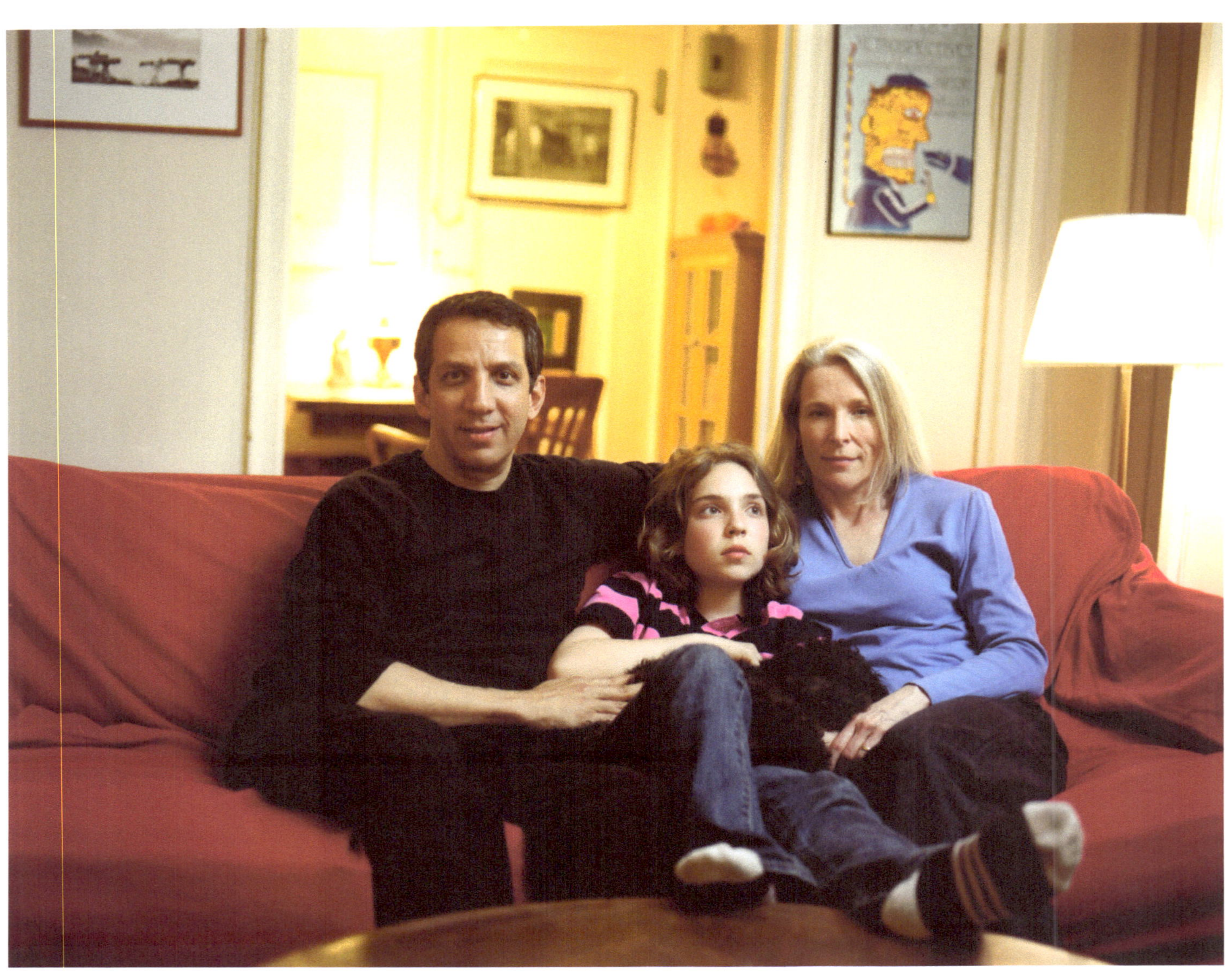

GABE, KATE, & EMILY

You could accurately say that many thousands of miles made up the route leading finally to the comfortable living room where this couple and young daughter sit contentedly together. Raised in Chicago and Cleveland, Gabe came to New York for a job that didn't happen and, as an alternative, put himself through art school, his true aim and interest anyhow. When art school came to an end—brilliantly, it should be noted—he had a year left of eligibility for a Eurail Pass, and, like many a painter and artist before him, he traveled through the capitals and museums of Europe, his sketching materials at the ready. By this time, Kate had left Washington, DC, finished college, and had determined that she, too, would make use of the resources of Europe—in her case by living and working in Madrid for whatever length of time it took for her to become fluent in Spanish. On her birthday, in Madrid, in the Prado, somewhere among the Goyas (one imagines these details instead of knowing them, although it really was in Madrid and it really was on her birthday), the paths of the two finally crossed. Further traveling went on for some weeks, but now with two travelers together, not one alone. A day came when Gabe posed a question. One autumn afternoon, of blue sky and warm air, in a sidewalk café along the Dalmatian coast, he sketched a view of the street he lived on in New York. Then he sketched a floor plan of the apartment he lived in, room by room, door by door, and window by window, right down to the sofa where it stood in the living room.

And there they are, to this day.

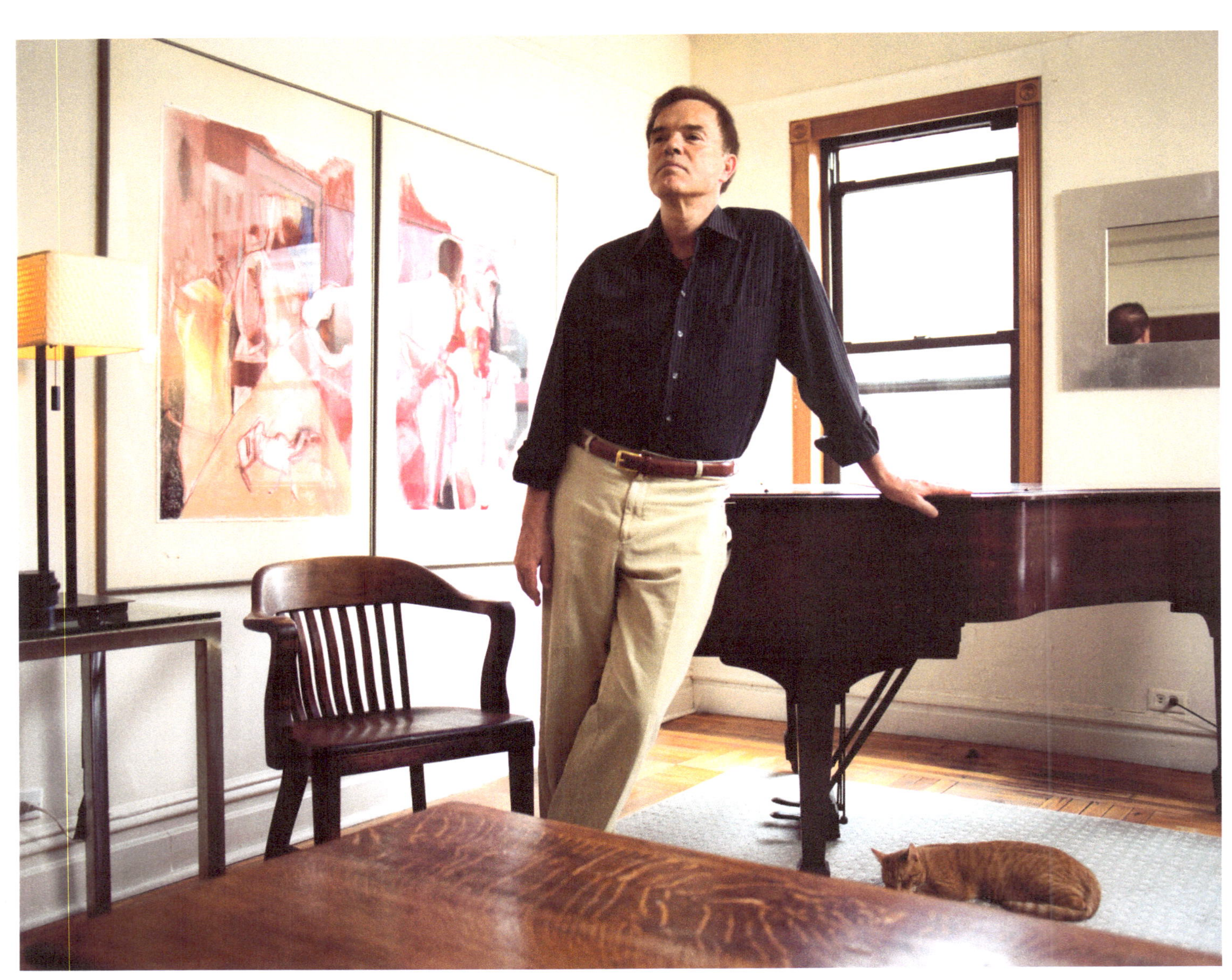

Commendatore in Don Giovanni,
Truffaldino in Adriadne auf Naxos,
Alfonso in Cosi fan Tutte,
Basilio in Il Barbiere di Siviglia.

GERHARDT

Gerhardt—or Gary, except on record liners and program notes—is a man so poised and witty, so confident in his savoir-faire, and so talented—that people might wonder where such a person came from. Answer: Ten or twelve blocks uptown.

His parents—ambitious academically, adventurous intellectually, bohemian temperamentally—were students at Columbia University when Gary first stirred into life, his parents seeing no reason to follow the convention of marriage until much later. When you try to think into the past, you confront the difficulty of imagining Gary as a young boy, an adolescent, and so on. His projection as a grown man is one of such comfortable self-reliance that it's as though he must be a person who simply came into being fully grown rather than having emerged out of earlier stages.

Whatever life with parents and siblings was like, it must have been rich with things of interest, intellect, and stimulation. College for Gary wasn't at conservatory, though he did take some courses there. Even so, almost the moment after graduation, he set forth as a performing bass-baritone and grew to be increasingly in demand.

Commendatore in *Don Giovanni*, Truffaldino in *Ariadne auf Naxos,* Alfonso in *Così fan tutte*, Basilio in *Il Barbiere di Siviglia,* Esc famillo in *Carmen, Ramphis in Aida,* the title role in Händel's *Giulio Cesare* along with many other roles both in the U.S. and Europe.

Would his fellow tenants know all this? Not many. Most would know him as the tenant from a high floor who punned in the elevator and bent down to converse with little kids. A good raconteur, Gary is fond of telling about the tenant on his floor long ago who'd had a pet ocelot: "Yes," he explains, "an ocelot—a small tiger." Once, when Gary was dog-sitting for a friend's beagle, the two apartment doors opened at the same time. Result? "The ocelot leapt into the hall and attacked the beagle. A dreadful scene," recalls Gary, "but somehow no serious harm came to anyone." The other tenant soon moved out.

From then to now, from *Ariadne* to ocelot, from the illustrious to the mundane. Gary, retired now from singing, has traveled them all—and still does, in his own unique and inestimable ways.

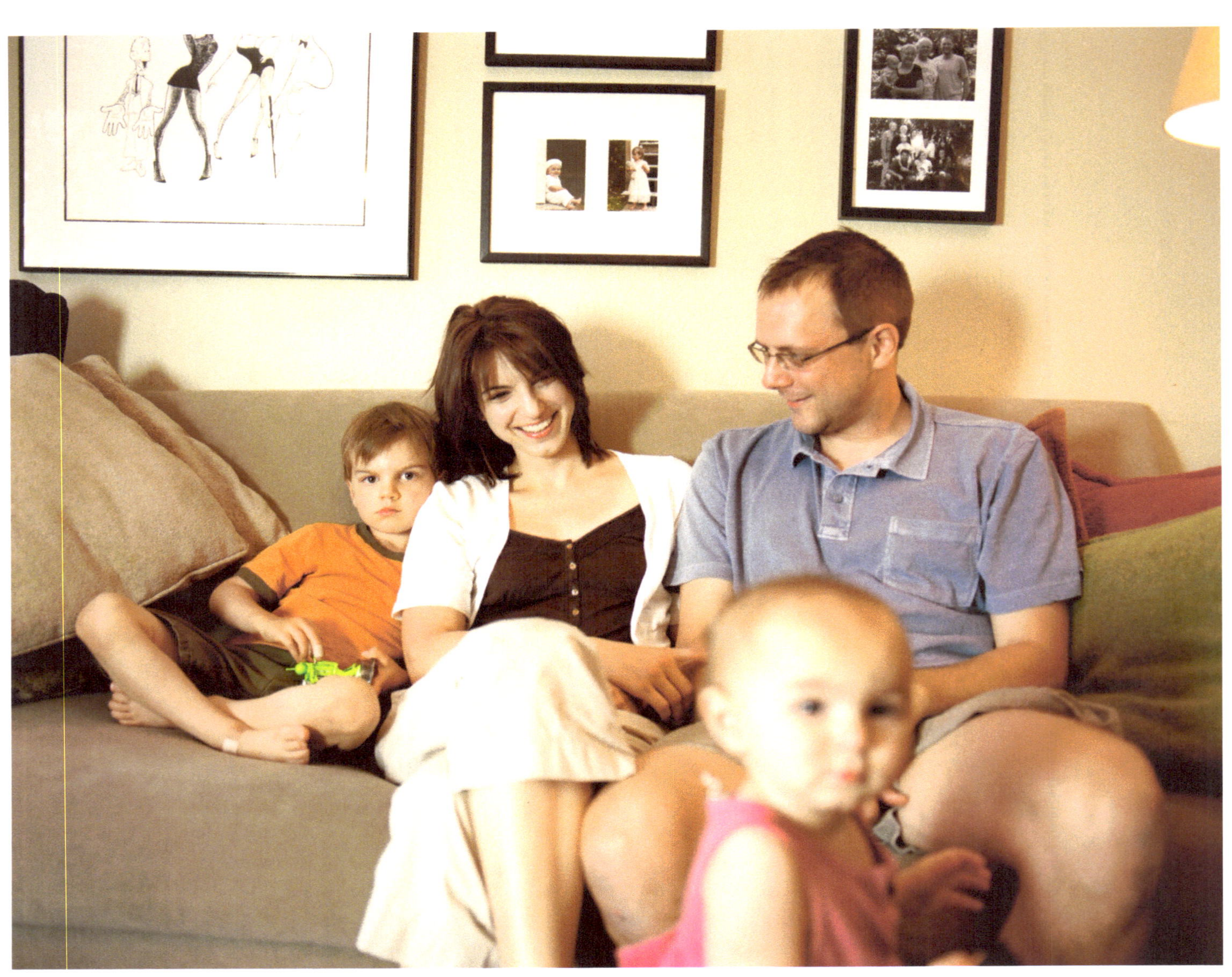

ROBYN, ANDY, EVAN, & TESS

Robyn came first. She signed the lease and for a handful of years shared the apartment with two or three other young women who had also found jobs in the city. This was in the early 1990s. Robyn's own job, teaching junior high, was actually not in town but forty-five minutes up the Saw Mill River Parkway. Every morning at seven sharp she would stop in at the little place on Broadway called "Tacuba" for a coffee to take along on the drive.

Almost no one who met Robyn failed to love her—including the tall and extraordinarily affable young man named Andy, who more and more often came by to visit at the building. Nothing with Robyn and Andy happened quickly, but instead things happened quietly, with a kind of poise and understatement, so that you didn't notice changes were taking place until they had already happened.

Robyn's apartment mates, one by one, fell away and disappeared. Then, more or less without anyone's noticing, Andy replaced them.

Almost no one who met Andy failed to like him—so when little Evan also "moved into" the apartment, and especially when he proved to be a miniature dead ringer for his father, it was a matter of delight for just about everyone.

Then the wonderful Tess also "moved in," and the little family was perfect. Even Robyn's teaching job was in the city now. But the apartment was growing smaller, or seemed to be, and the rent was growing larger, as were the children, although Parker, the almost goofily friendly dog, stayed pretty much the same size as ever.

Then Robyn's job in the city fell apart, and her new post turned out to be in Connecticut. Andy, a writer, could work anywhere, but Robyn's commute meant that she had hardly any time to spend with the children. And so, with one such thing and another, the family moved away. They left like swallows, quietly and quickly. They were nowhere to be seen, and they left a very deep emptiness behind them.

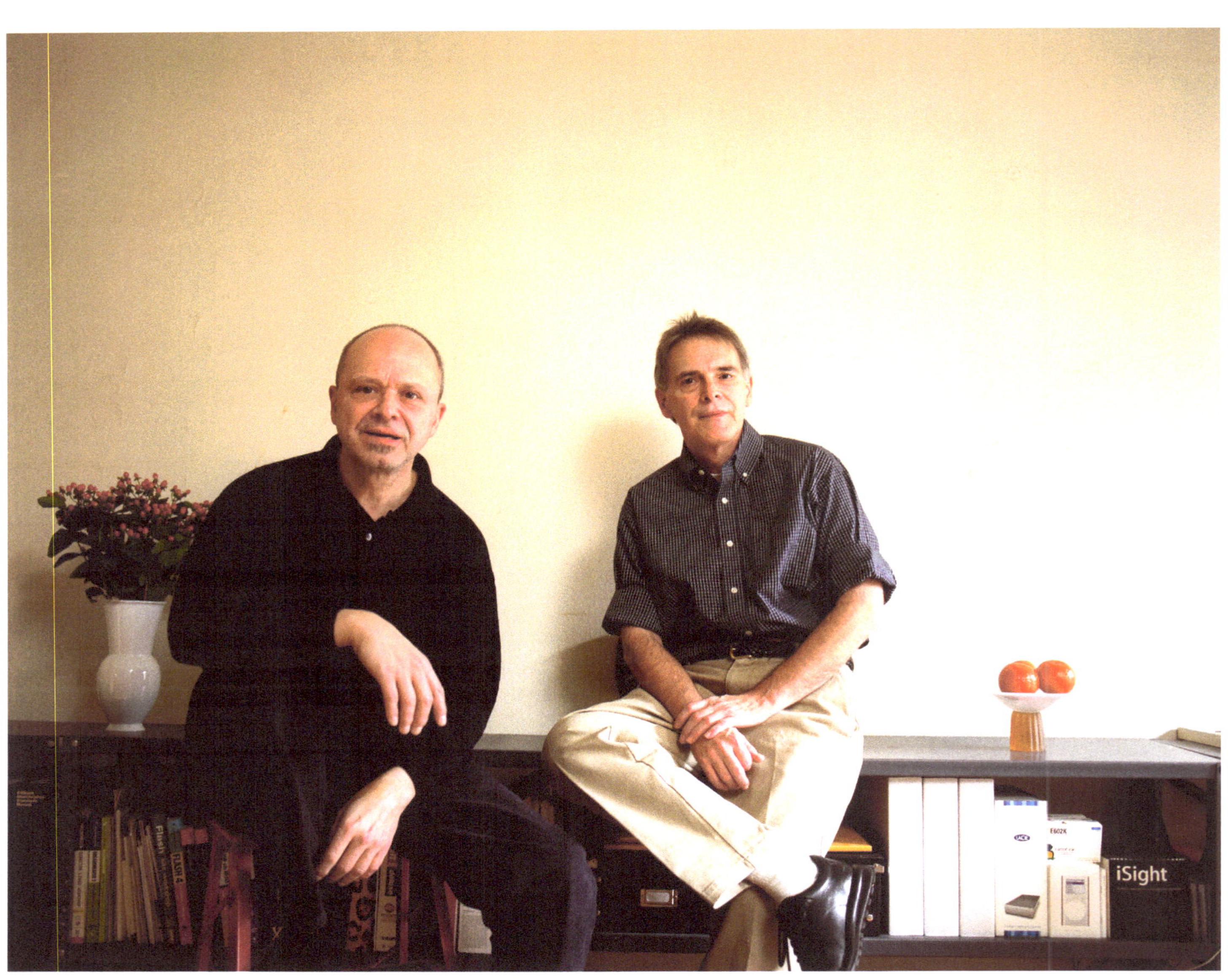

ROSS & TOM

What words, do you suppose, would come to mind if someone who knew them well considered Ross and Tom? "Skillful," certainly, "gifted," and then also "wry," "detached," and "quizzical." But problems arise immediately: "Detached," for example. It urgently needs qualification, since neither one of these enormously talented men who've been tenants in the building for decades is in the least bit detached in the sense of "aloof," "superior" or "having airs." Two plainer or more generous and considerate people you couldn't find. In fact, let's allow "detached" to give way altogether to the "observant" we used a minute ago, along with a couple of other words, like "discriminating," "thoughtful," maybe even "percipient."

Hailing from different parts of the eastern seaboard, Ross and Tom are both graphic designers, and splendidly gifted ones at that. They met when they found themselves working side by side at a fiercely competitive firm where the question wasn't whether you would last (no one did), but how long you would last. They did well on the longevity test, and when the inevitable end did come, Tom went to a teaching post and Ross to another design position. Tom had been in the building for several years before he met Ross—and was owner of a huge, gentle, rust-red, long-haired dog named Romulus that was loved by every child in the building.

Back to words, though. Look at the pensive, measuring, thoughtful expression on Tom's face (he's on the right). And then at the borderline mischievous expression on Ross's. A fitting word for Ross could be "puckish," with his droll, quick, and sharp sense of humor. Tom seems slightly the more pensive—until you talk with him a while and find he's just as quick-witted and lightning-minded as Ross.

Or what if they weren't words but punctuation marks? Well, exclamation points, certainly, for laughter, quickness, and drollery. Semi-colons for the subtlety of their associations, and then dashes and hyphens for afterthoughts—first—and for joined thoughts—second. But no end-stops. Who could want Ross and Tom to stop?

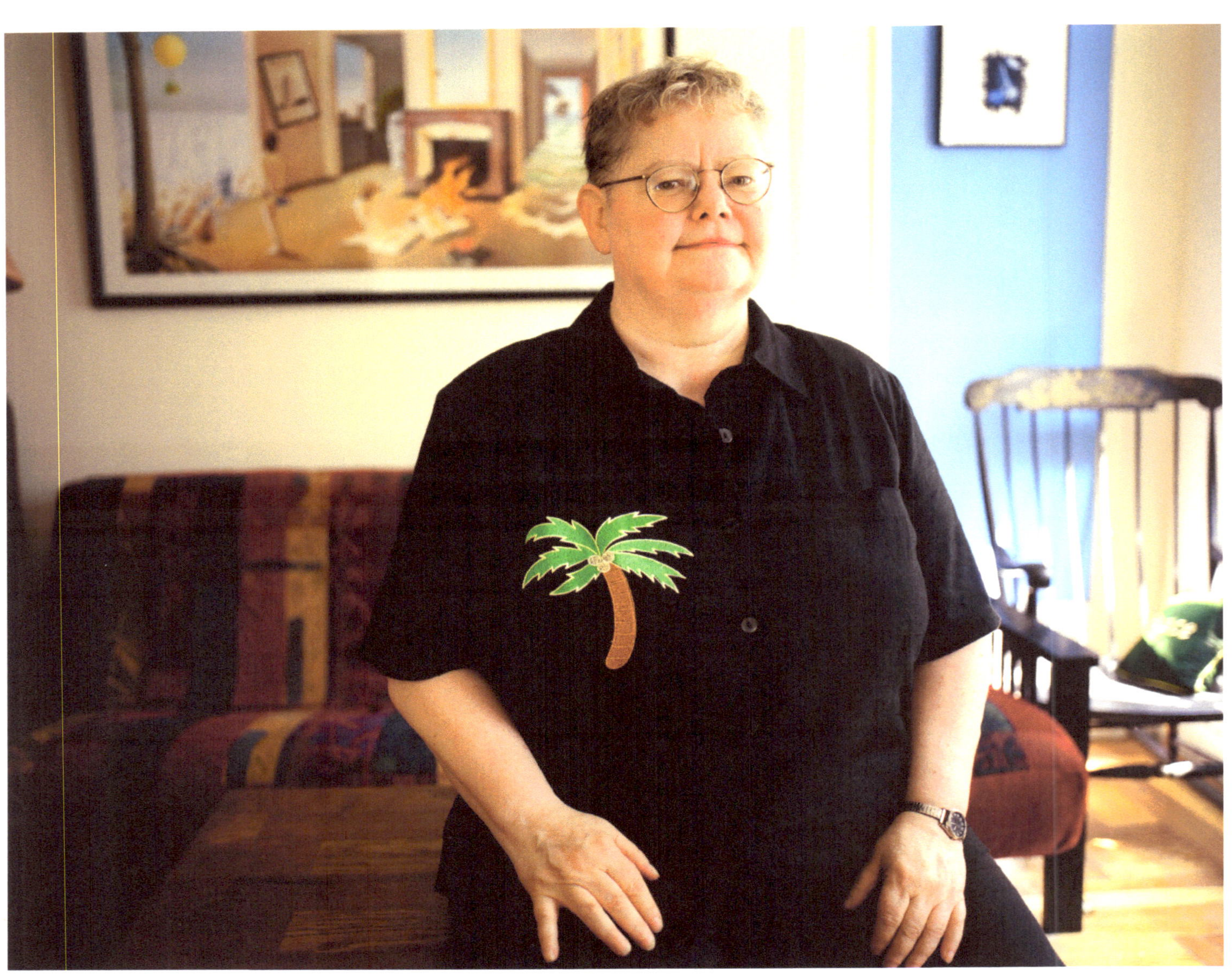

TESS & CHRISTINE

Tess says that she moved into the building "over several years," and she's not exaggerating. Born and raised on the West Coast, she moved to the middle of the country and brought to near-completion a Ph.D. in Chinese history—truncated only when social justice caught her energies and she took up labor organizing. Her next stop was New York, though still not at the address of this building. In 1980, though, she met Christine, who did live in the building (and had since 1963), and, over the next several years, more and more of Tess's "stuff" found its way to—and remained in—Christine's apartment. In 1987, the two agreed to make Tess's move permanent, and from the very start, Tess says, it felt like home—in part because Christine made real home-made meals, a big plus for the non-cooking Tess. With the good times came sorrow, too, when Christine was badly injured in a traffic accident and never fully recovered. Twelve years later, she died, and Tess began all over again—without Christine.

Labor work gave way to law school, law school led to a degree, and the degree led to a practice. For a long time, Tess had the companionship of her little dog, and she often worried—"I'm a fretter," she says; "I fret"—how, if there were ever a fire, she would manage to climb down her rope ladder while also holding the dog. Luckily, no such challenge ever arose.

Tess still doesn't cook. A few years back, Con Ed was making some major repairs and shut off gas to the building. Later they came around to each apartment, checking for air in the lines. When they opened the lid of Tess's stove, they—and Tess—saw a very well-cooked mouse. Who needs gas anyway? thought Tess, and left the valve forever shut. She microwaves a bit, but mainly she orders in.

Tess crossed the continent to reach apartment 6D, where she found happiness, then great sorrow, and then the ability to forge happiness of a new kind.

Tess is a true keeper.

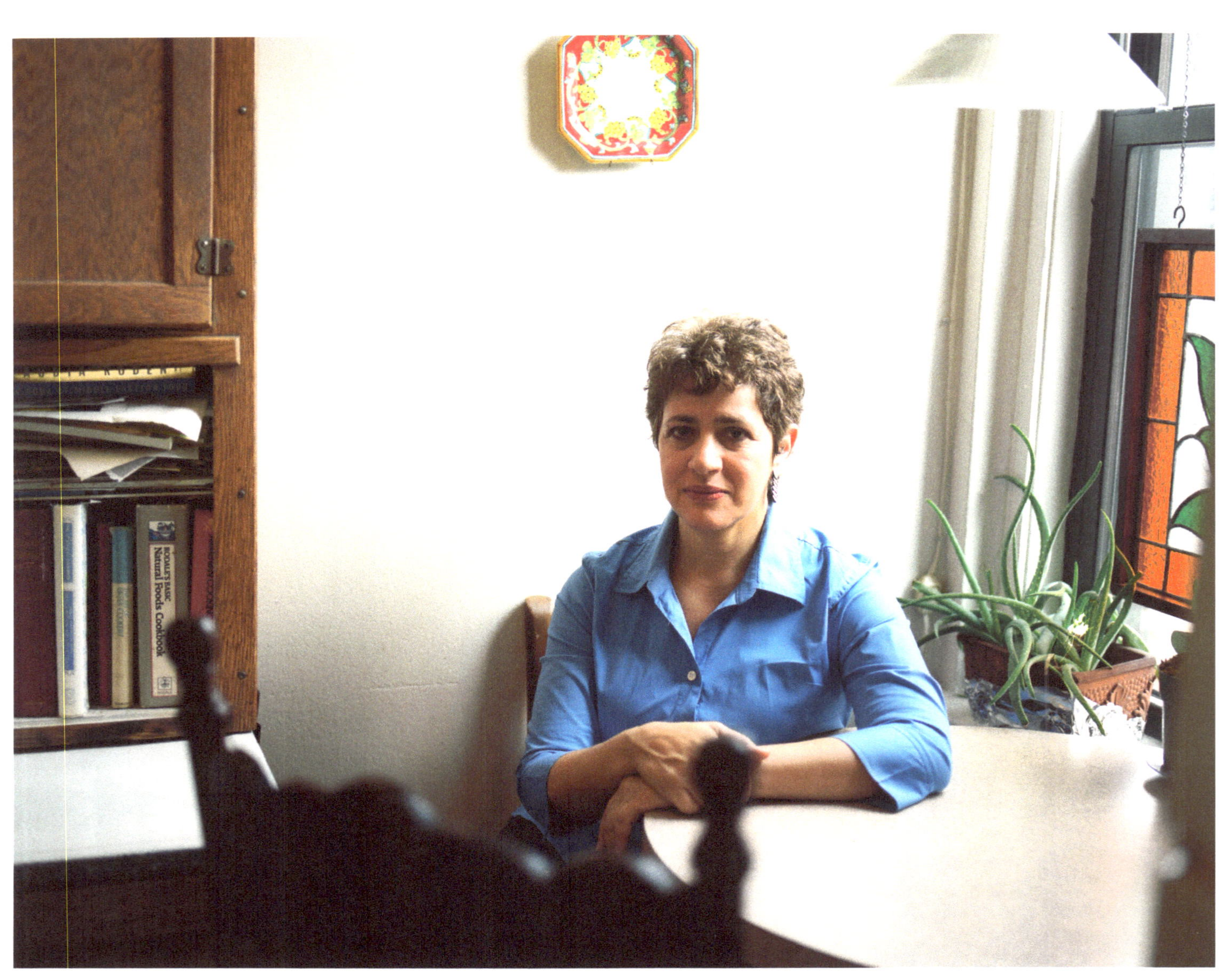

Her image — its balance and poise,
stillness, color and light —

ZOYA

Zoya's roots, reaching back to Armenia, tie three centuries together. They lead from Armenia to Cyprus, then from Cyprus to London, where her father moved as an architecture student. From London, Zoya's roots—but not yet Zoya—cross the Atlantic to New Jersey, and there Zoya begins. Once grown, she crossed the river to Manhattan, a marriage, and, toward the end of that marriage, to the apartment house she now lives in, the table she sits at, and to the window that allows the light to fall across her face. Her image—its balance and poise, stillness, color and light—might almost have been painted by Vermeer.

In 1895, or very close to it, Zoya's paternal grandfather was five years old. An Armenian christening party was being celebrated in a building out in the countryside. At one point, the young boy needed the bathroom, and, because darkness was falling, an older cousin escorted him across the garden to the outhouse. During the time they were there, a band of Turks came. The band harassed the guests, then killed them all and burned the building to its foundation—as two terrified boys watched through a crack in the outhouse wall. Zoya's grandfather, the five-year-old, was taken to Cyprus. There, in 1911, Zoya's father was born.

Her parents met in wartime London (their wedding cake was a cardboard cylinder covered with frosting). Her brother was born there. Her father shipped out as an English soldier while mother and son remained in London during the Blitz. Her mother worked in an office. Every few days another desk or two would become vacant. Zoya was born ten months after the family's arrival in the U.S.

Her career has been in theater, production, design, and stage managing. The work is demanding, a lot of travel is required, and Zoya has been doing it for a long time. When asked, once, what keeps her going, she thought for a moment. Then she told about a time when she'd watched one of her shows, *The Miracle Worker,* from a seat in the house. At the final curtain, a man near her was weeping—quietly but plentifully and unashamedly. That sort of thing, Zoya said, helps keep her going.

He and the group walked only
in the dark hours, night
after night for weeks...

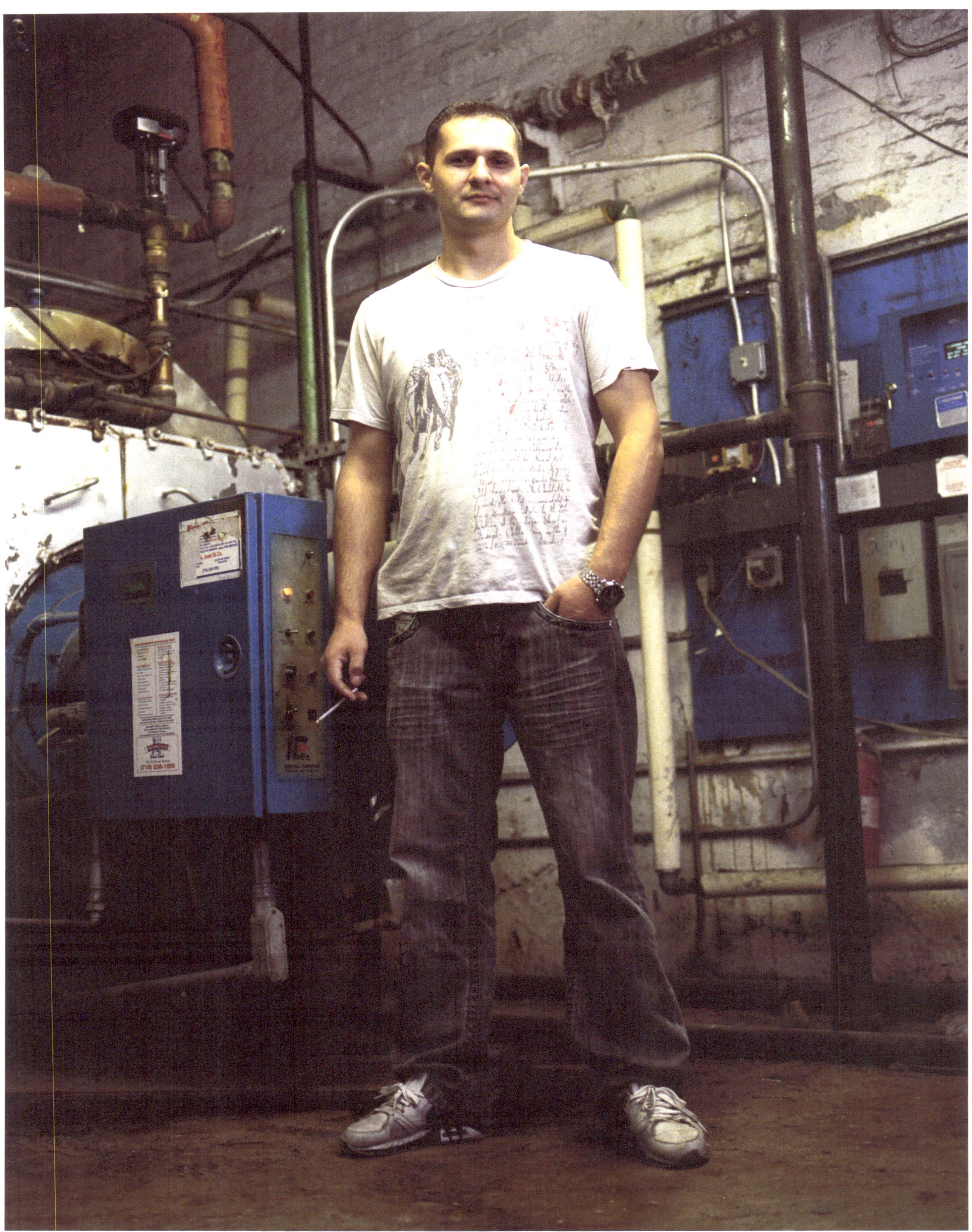

VIC

Already he has come and gone, the super known to everyone as Vic, although that wasn't even close to his real first name. In the boiler room portrait, his age is twenty-eight. Just after his twentieth birthday, he joined a group of thirty or so other young men intent on getting secretly out of their native Kosovo—as it happened, not long in advance of the bombings and huge displacements of people that were to take place soon after.

Vic and the group walked only in the dark hours, night after night for weeks, using the daytimes for hiding and rest. Getting food and water was a matter of luck, opportunity, and sometimes secret charity. The men crossed Serbia, crossed Hungary, stole into Slovakia, then from there into to the Czech Republic. The border into Germany was trickier. Vic and those remaining in the group were caught by the German border patrol and jailed for two weeks before being released back into the Czech Republic. The same thing happened again. On the third try, they made it undetected into Germany.

Vic studied. He learned German. He applied to a program of admission to the United States for people under twenty-one—and got accepted three days before his twenty-first birthday. In New York, just as in Germany, he studied. He learned English. His parents were in the city already, and he worked with his father in building maintenance. He took courses in technical schools, qualified himself in maintenance of all four types of residential boilers. He applied for U.S. citizenship. He got it.

After having been in the building for just under two years, he moved on. Anyone who came to know Vic at all well—including his great sense of humor—also knows that his trajectory is far from over.

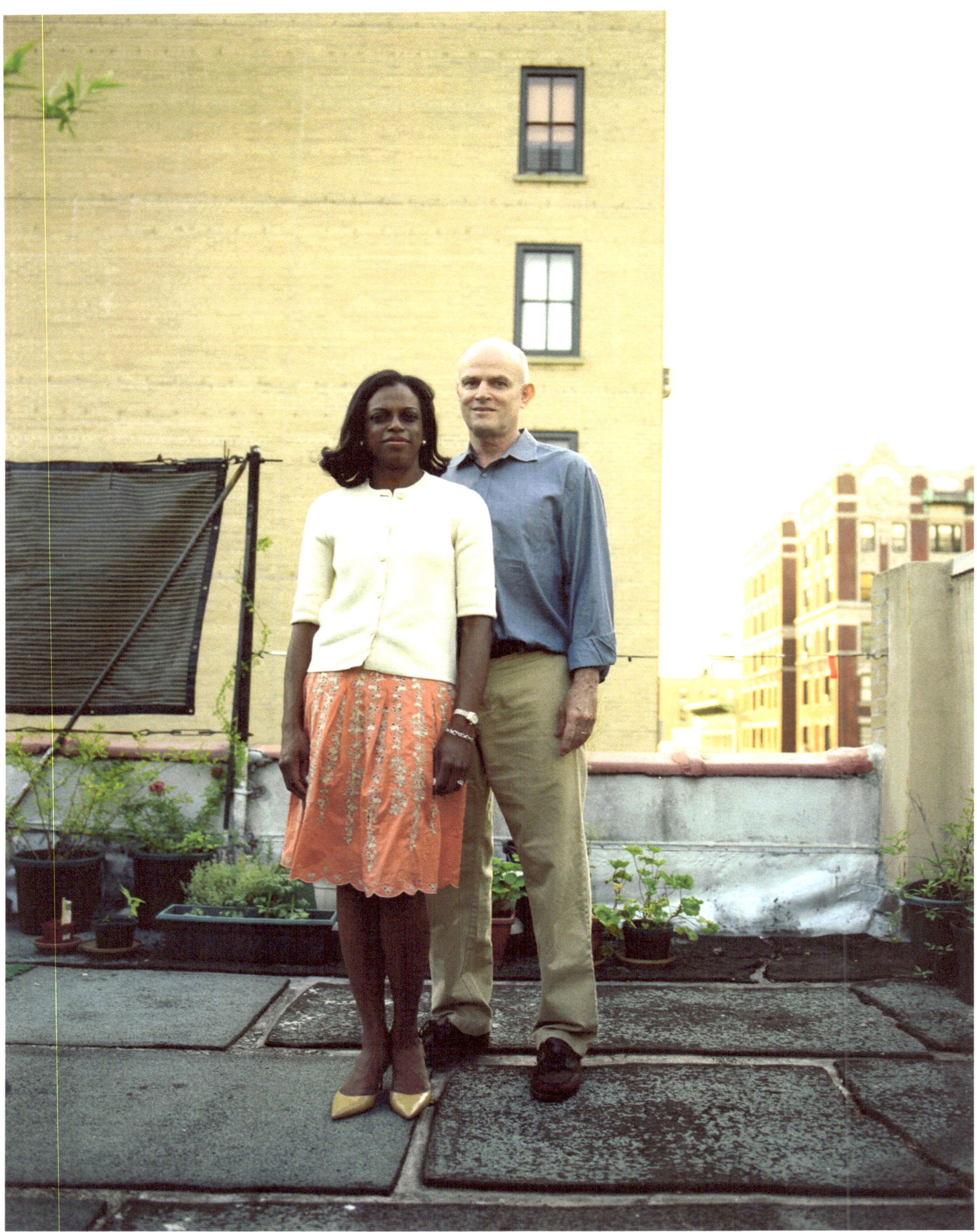

MATT & GELSEY

Gary, the professional bass-baritone who, long ago, encountered the ocelot—once referred to Matt and Gelsey as the building's "elegance at the top," the "top," of course, meaning penthouse. A class act himself, Gary's metaphor was a more genuine gift than it might have been from another.

Matt has lived in the building much longer than Gelsey, though their getting together as a couple dates now from nearly a decade ago. Matt, though, was a tenant all the way back in the 1970s. On the night of July 13, 1977, when the lights went out all across New York City—arson, crime, and looting snarling out from the folds of darkness—I remember groping our way down the east stairwell, my wife and I and our daughters of three and six—and bumping into Matt and a handful of friends groping their way up. Our reason for groping down was to find out what had happened—meaning, in major part, to see if we could get hold of some batteries to make a dead portable radio come alive. Matt said, "Don't go out. Stay home. I might have some batteries." We did go home, and soon afterward Matt was at our door bearing batteries that allowed us to tune in to the immensity of what was happening. Later, as we looked out our windows, car headlights swept across the Stygian blackness of the intersection at Broadway as cars, chains tied to their bumpers, swerved and revved to pull gratings off of storefronts.

Now, Matt has retired from a long career in labor law. Part of this couple's elegance lies in their complete freedom from any trace of falseness or affectation. Even with her great beauty and high sense of style, Gelsey is never other than direct, plain, and friendly. Matt, whose politics are so deeply rooted in a populist interpretation of justice as to put him more to the left than most people could imagine—even with so enveloping a set of principles, Matt is invariably the model of politeness, consideration for others, and, not least, modesty.

What's wrong with Matt and Gelsey? What can be found to say about them that's bad? Maybe in the next edition of this book there will be something like that to include. Or, more likely, not. Let's just say, for now, that they're human. And add a wish that all the population of earth could be a model of these two.

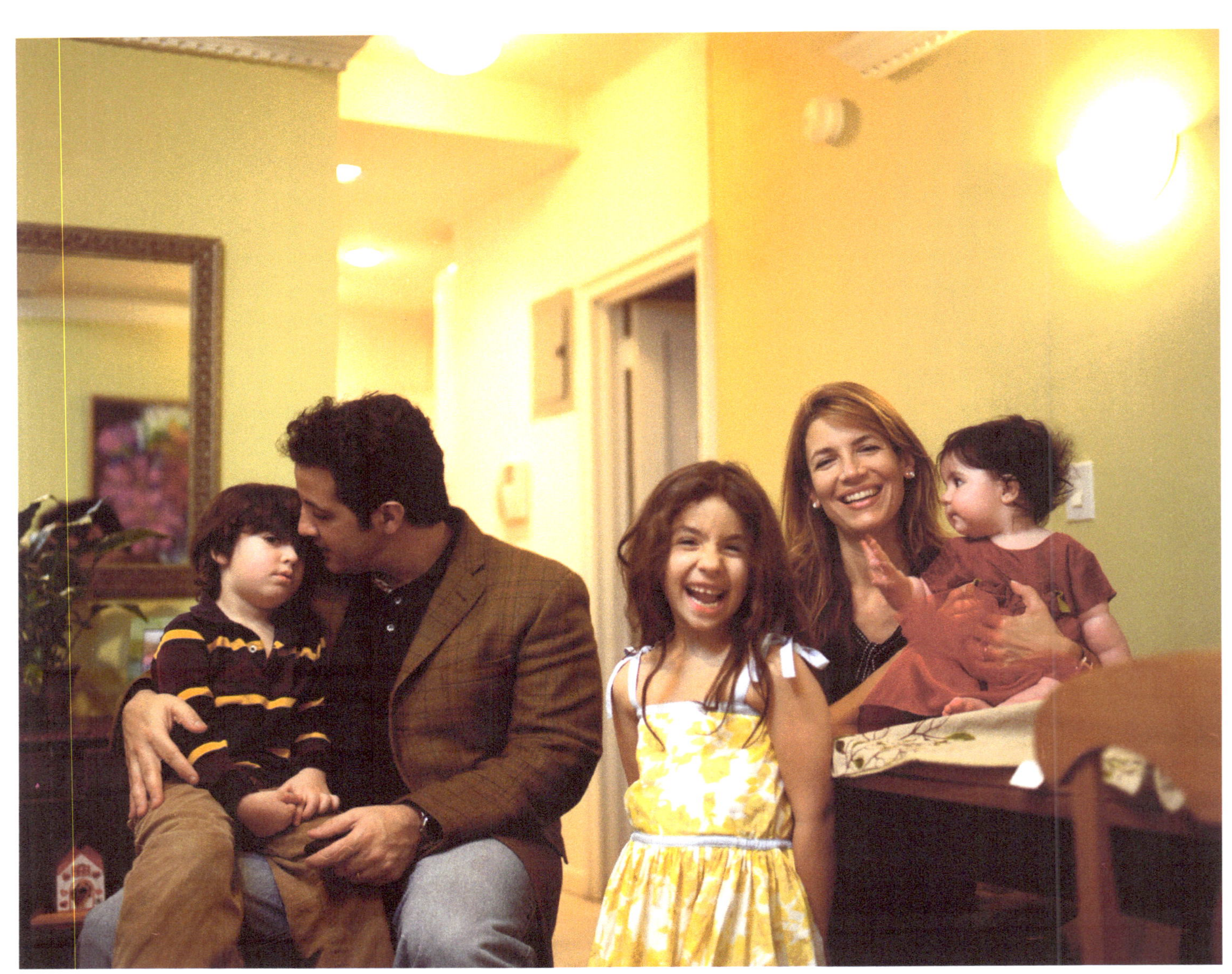

Now, how different it is,
Three growing children
push hard at life, and at time.

CATHERINE, DAVID, SYDNEY, ANDREW, & SIENA

There are times when history changes much more quickly than at others, or seems to. One such time is when children are young. This portrait of the Merrill family, for example: By the time you look at it—whenever that moment is—Sydney, Andrew, and Siena will be very different young people than they were here. Consider that between reaching three years of age and six, a child goes through half of life as he or she has lived it up to that point. In reaching twenty from ten, the same thing happens. But then begins the slowing down: Going to thirty from twenty is only a fifty-percent repeat, sixty-five from sixty is a repeat of only one-twelfth. No wonder time slows as we age. Or, looking at it the other way, no wonder it speeds up so dreadfully.

It depends on which way you look at it, but either way there's a difference, and it's enormous. David and Catherine reached New York by a sort of caliper movement: Catherine arrived from Boston, David from Washington, D.C. They met in New York—and stayed, both in the city and together.

When they became a family of five, they ended up living in Mrs. Engel's old apartment, although admittedly it was much altered—and the pace of time became altogether different there from what it had been through the creeping decades of Mrs. Engel's solitary existence inside the same walls. When Mrs. Engel was here, nothing but silence, for days at a time, would emerge through the front door into the hall, and no children's voices, like now, would rise through open windows into the air. Decades ago, you might come upon Mrs. Engel nursing the elevator door open from inside, pushing at it timidly with her folded white tissue. Now, how different it is. Three growing children push hard at life, and at time.

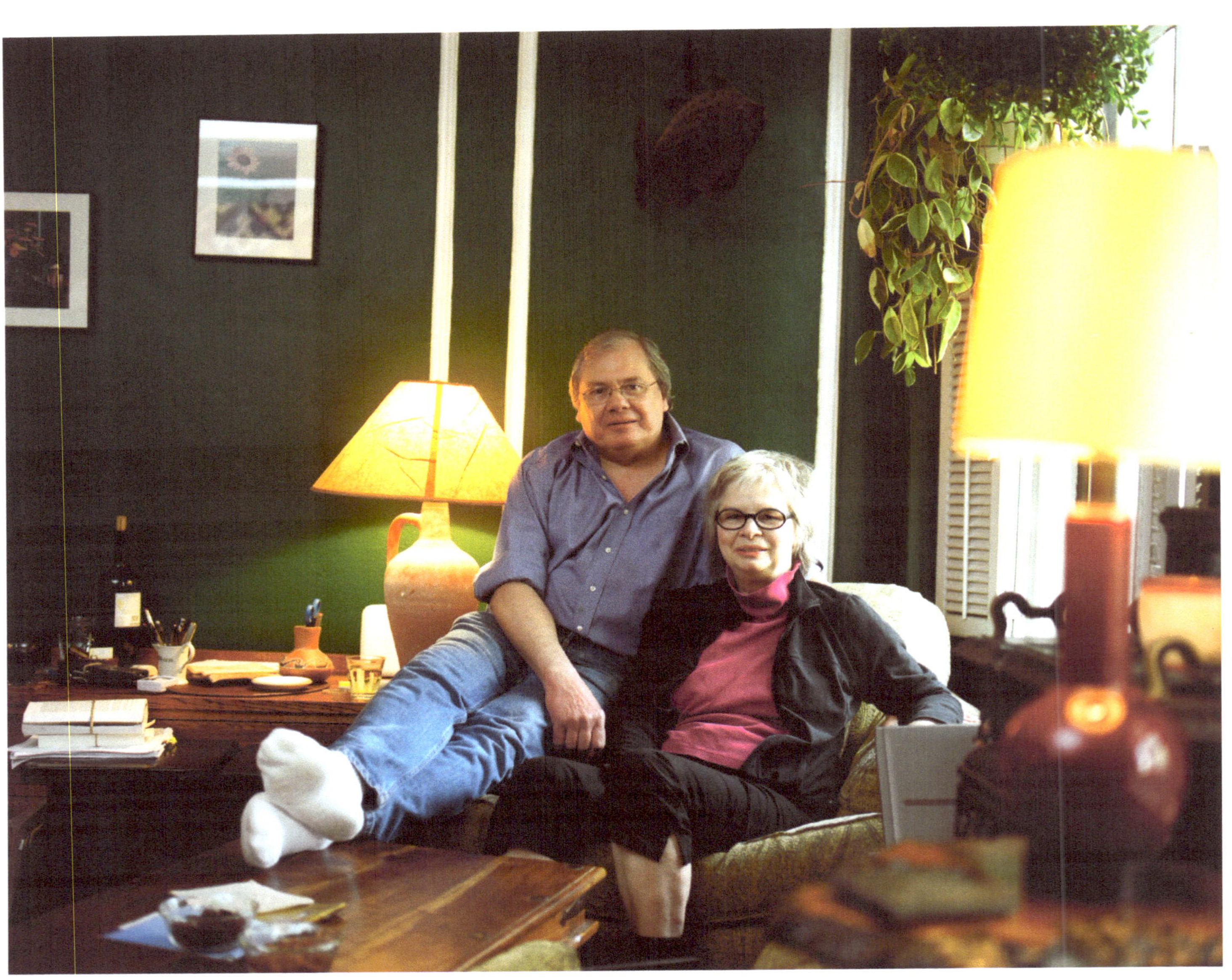

MALCOLM & ZOË

One summer morning forty years ago, Malcolm and Zoë Reiner waited in this same room—it was otherwise entirely empty—for a trucker from the Bronx to ring the buzzer and start bringing up their "stuff." There was an ironing board, a collapsible butterfly chair, some pots and pans, a few kitchen utensils packed away, a small number of dishes nested in crumpled paper. A sewing machine. And books, twenty or twenty-five boxes of them.

Malcolm and Zoë had no idea that four decades later they would still be in the same place—the same apartment, same living room with the same windows, looking over the same street. An entire span of life has gone by, somehow. In the beginning, time passed gradually, and then it went faster and faster. Malcolm and Zoë were thirty when they moved in. Now they are seventy.

Where did they go, all those years? Books, furniture, guests, recipes, meals, vacations, expeditions, snowstorms, holidays—all of these were markers, large and small, that showed time passing, but the true mileposts in the narrative of the decades were created by the lives of Zoë and Malcolm's children. Their first child was born before the living room had a stick of furniture in it—only boxes filled with books. Her sister was born three years later. Everything in life seemed to be measured by the stages of their growth.

Even now, artifacts remain in the apartment, things left behind from the many years. In one closet are boxes of children's books; in another, there's a cache of toys and games—a castle, an entire town of Smurfs, a collection of matchbox cars. Elsewhere, a pair of shoes for a two-year-old, two or three small sweaters, a few other pieces of clothing that seem to hold antiquity itself about them, even though they're not as old as the people who wore them.

There are occasions when, almost without her knowing it, Zoë's mind threads its way back to one particular moment or another in the past. Sometimes, when this happens, a darkness seems to steal up from behind her and throw her into shock. It's as if her breath has been snatched away, and she is left gasping.

Where did they go, she asks, all those moments, days, and times? What happened?

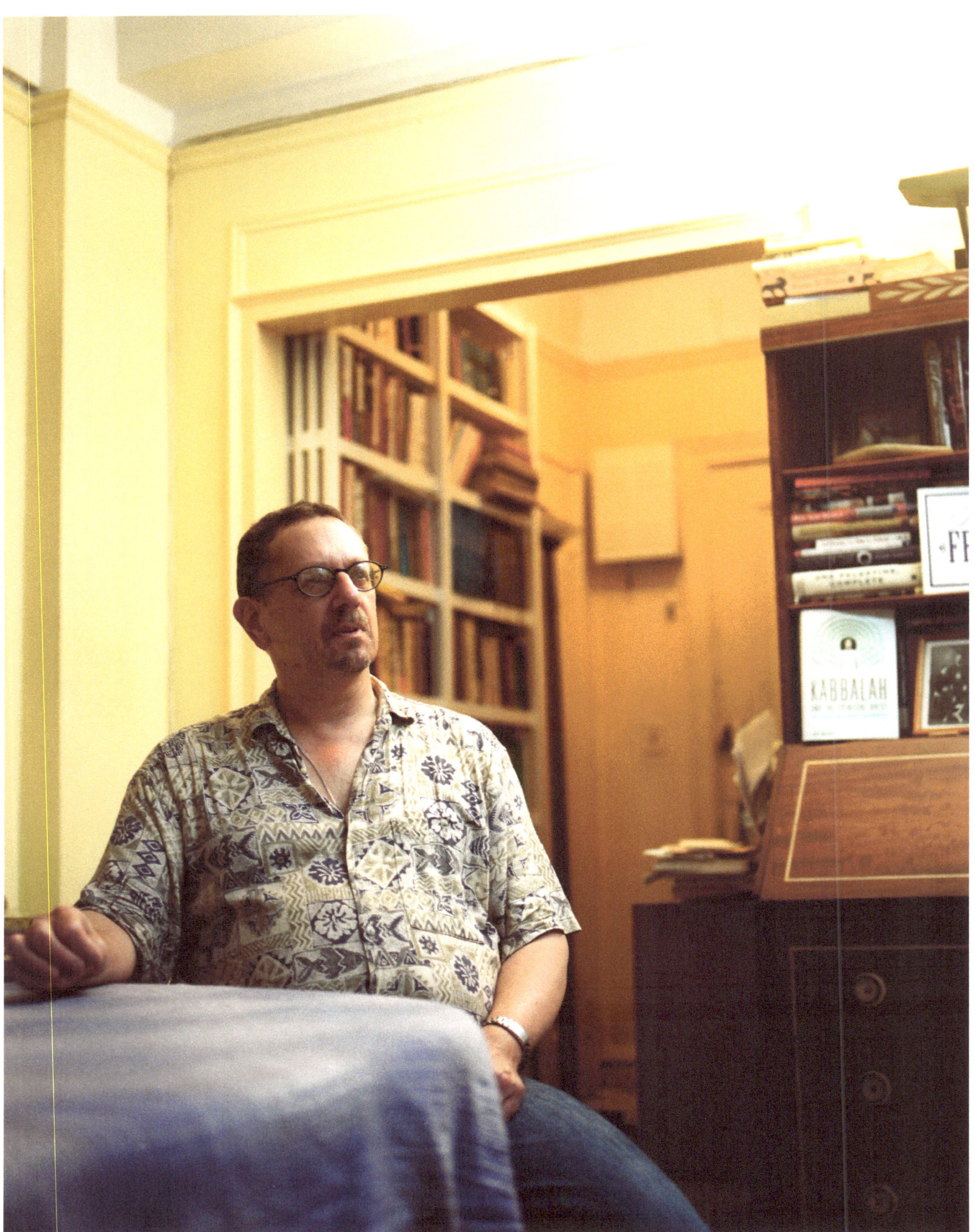

ELI

It almost seems as though time has no effect on Eli. Unlike with other people, it passes around him, while he himself remains unchanged. Perhaps he holds the past inside him.

He came to the building in the middle 70s and moved into an apartment at the back. Marrying afterward, he and his wife produced a lovely and talented daughter who is now, more than a quarter of a century later, grown and gone off to a life of her own. In her early childhood, this daughter especially charmed and enchanted one of the tenants on the same floor, the older man known to almost everyone in the building as "Mr. Ernst." He doted on the girl, reveling in her as she grew. Very late in life, Mr. Ernst married a woman near his own age whose first husband had died in Europe, in the Holocaust. This was a fact well known to Eli.

Too soon, Mr. Ernst's wife grew ill and passed away. A tiny handful of years later so did Mr. Ernst. By this time, Eli's own marriage had ended and his wife had moved away from the building as well.

Throughout all these departures, changes, and absences, Eli himself remained unchanged, or changed so little that it went unnoticed or seemed no change at all. So many others had moved on, in one way or another. Still, the spirit of the house seems to cling to them, and to memory of them, so long as Eli remains where he is.

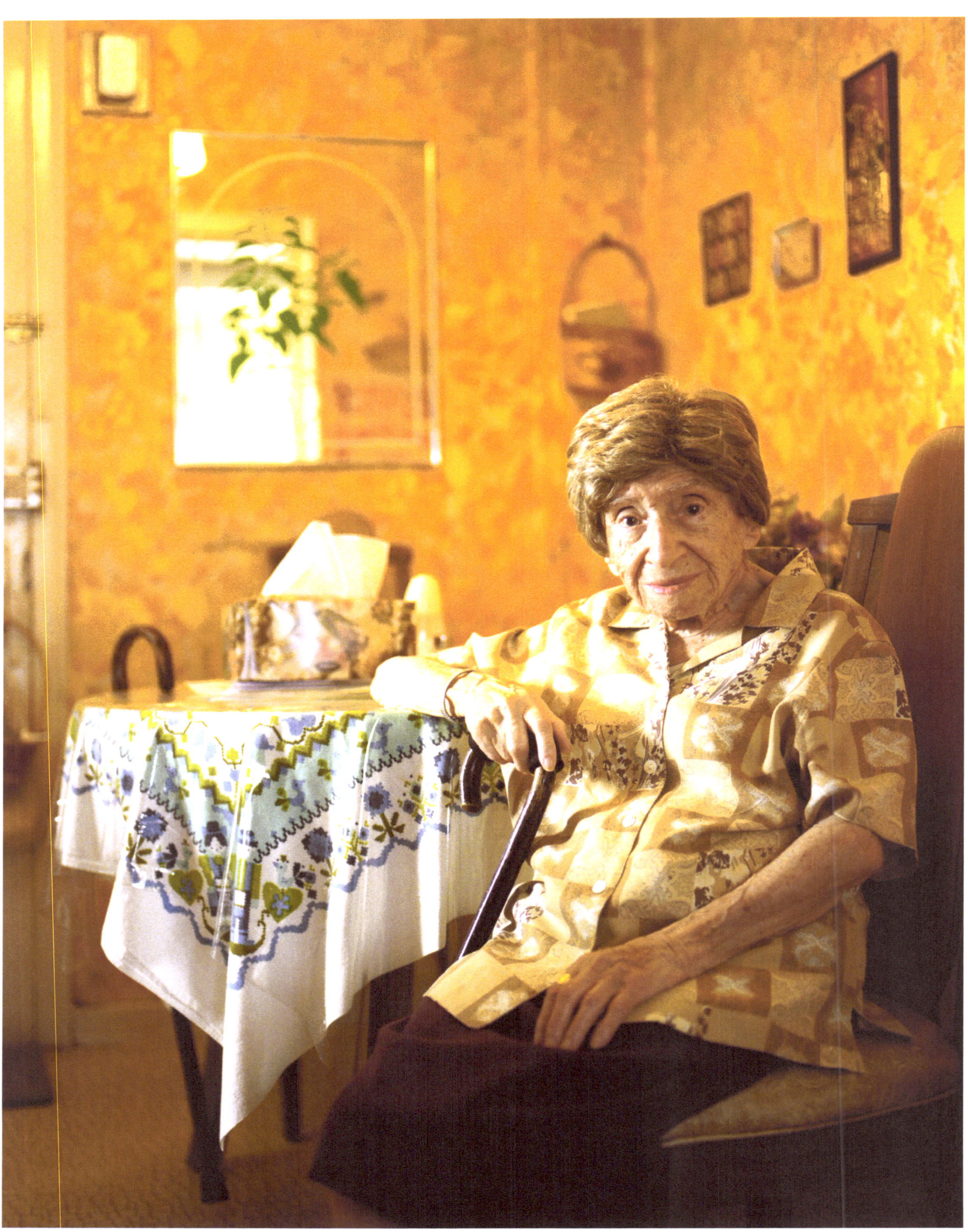

MRS. IRIT TEMKIN

Only close friends called her "Irit." To everyone else, she was "Mrs. Temkin."

Before the end, she became the building's oldest tenant. She reached into history farther than anyone.

She was born in Antwerp in 1911. When World War I came and went, she was a schoolgirl, then a young woman during the years between that war and the next.

Irit was twenty-seven when she and other family members escaped to Marseilles, where it was promised that passports would be waiting. They were—but unsigned. New documents had to be arranged for—meaning a wait of two whole years in hiding. Two aunts and one uncle were exposed, taken, and destroyed by the Nazis. Irit learned French before she finally reached Lisbon. From there, she sailed to New York.

The older of her two sons has the passport she traveled on.

In New York, she met her future husband, whom she married in 1948. A diamond-cutter, he was from Poland, where before the war he'd been married with two children. Decades later, Irit's older son, after years of research, found proof that both the wife and children had perished at Treblinka, his own step-mother and half-siblings.

In New York, years passed. Money was scarce, housing crowded. In 1962, the family moved to apartment 6C—where both sons rejoiced at the luxury of actually having a bedroom.

More years passed. The sons went to college, left home. In 1986, Irit's husband died. She continued life alone, taking pleasure in grandchildren. Of a fellow tenant with two grown daughters, she invariably asked, "Are they married yet?"

Past two o'clock she rose from her bed, went down two flights and knocked at the back door of what had once been the apartment of her dear friend Klara Weilberg and family. It was now the apartment of Max Prechtel, who, up late working on a book, heard a faint knock. He opened the door and saw the tiny figure of Mrs. Temkin. Sweet, polite, unpresuming, earnest, she had gone, in the dead of the night, on a visit to the past.

Others, through Mrs. Temkin, made that same visit, in differing ways. But then she disappeared, this time entirely and forever, taking the past with her—except for the dustings of time and memory left on those who'd known her, the many whom in one way or another she had touched.

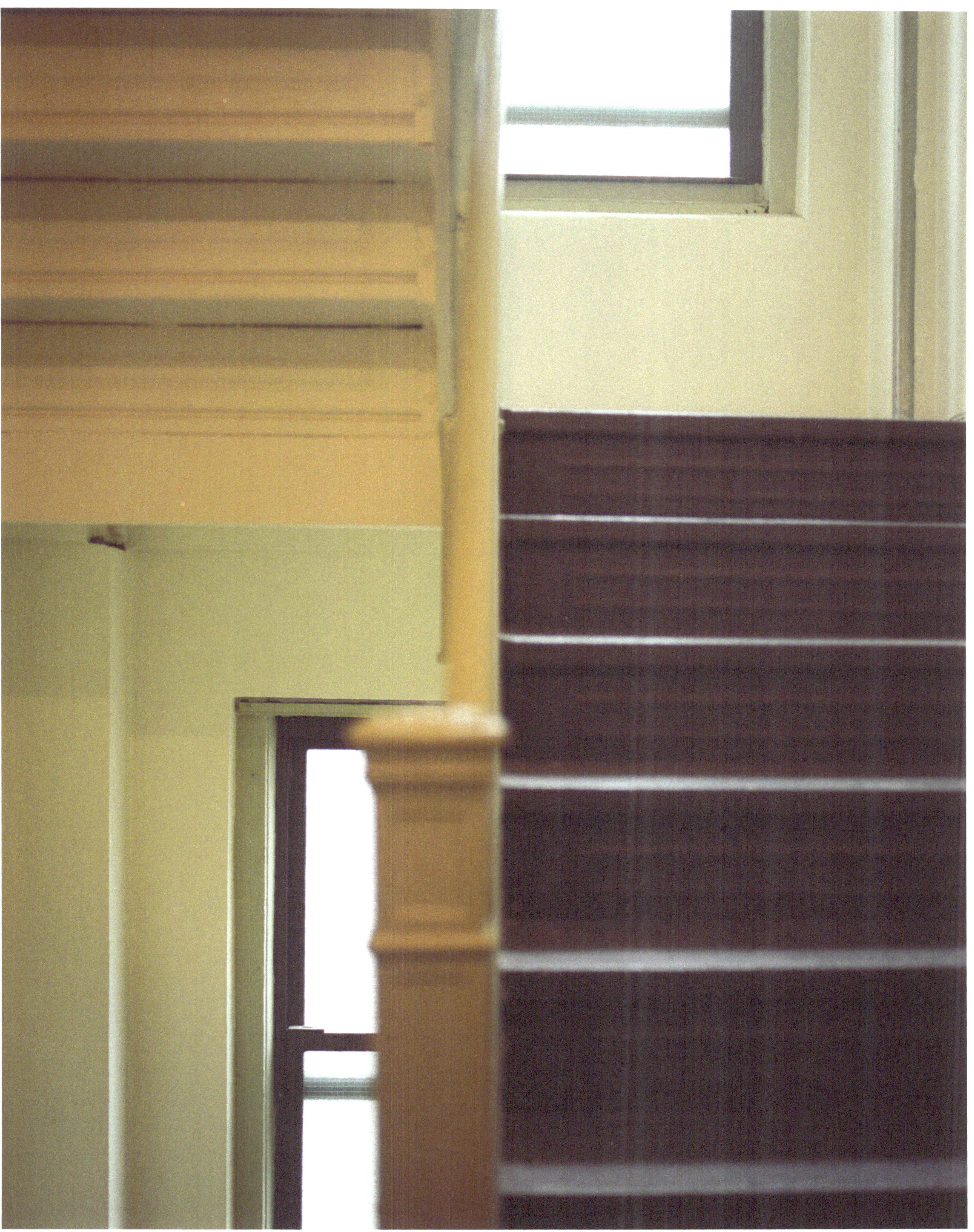

where did they go,
she asks, all those moments,
days and times?

Or what if these two were
punctuation marks? They'd be
exclamation points, certainly,
for laughter, quickness, and drollery.
Semi-colons for the subtlety of their
associations, then dashes and
hyphens for afterthoughts.

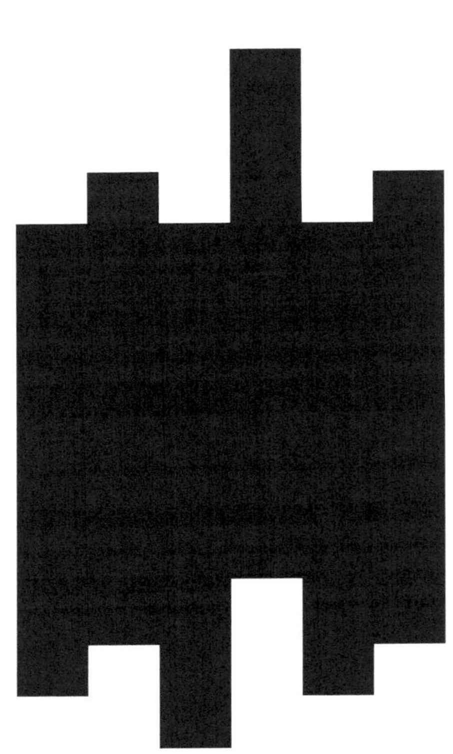